I0666916

An ARIA Anthology

SOMETHING
EXTRAORDINARY

Selected Short Fiction, Nonfiction, Poetry & Prose from
The Association of Rhode Island Authors

Something Extraordinary: Selected short fiction,
nonfiction, poetry & prose from The Association
of Rhode Island Authors; an ARIA Anthology
Copyright © 2025 Association of Rhode Island Authors.
Entries are copyright 2025 to their respective authors.

Produced and printed by Stillwater River Publications.
All rights reserved. Written and produced in the United States of America.
This book may not be reproduced or sold in any form without the expressed,
written permission of the author(s) and publisher.

Visit our website at www.StillwaterPress.com for more information.

First Stillwater River Publications Edition

ISBN: 978-1-965733-89-9

Library of Congress Control Number: 2025942693

12345678910
Publication of the Association of Rhode Island Authors (ARIA)
Published by Stillwater River Publications,
West Warwick, RI, USA.

*The views and opinions expressed in this book are
solely those of the author(s) and do not necessarily reflect
the views and opinions of the Association of Rhode
Island Authors (ARIA) or the publisher.*

Previous ARIA Anthologies

Contents

Foreword

To celebrate ARIA's tenth annual anthology, we chose 'Something Extraordinary' for the theme. Broad and wide open to interpretation, this theme challenged our talented authors and has brought forth a myriad of stories and poetry which I'm sure you will enjoy!

Something extraordinary goes above and beyond what is expected. This can be good or bad. Saving a child from a burning building is an extraordinary act of heroism, but a test score of 11 out of 100 is extraordinary, too. (Thanks, vocabulary.com)

What is extraordinary? For some, it's in their own family history. A tale of exceptional valor, heroism, even one's own unique journey through life fits the theme. Family played a leading role in many of these stories.

In fact, the story that received the highest average rating from our judges leads off this volume, as is tradition. And I couldn't be happier to congratulate perennial contributor Jack Nolan for writing such an exceptional essay. You can find more of Jack's noteworthy writing in our previous anthologies.

Extraordinary can be found even in the ordinary, right? There's a philosophy that when you take nothing for granted, life is abundant. It's spending each day consciously aware of the amazing things around you, as you'll find in Eric Crook's "Ollie," or the remarkable poem "seadevil" by Stephanie Nary.

You'll find short stories and poems here that will bring a smile, or a tear, but will resonate with you, as all good stories and poems should. I hope you treat this anthology as you would a good friend – relax, put your feet up, set your favorite beverage nearby, and happy reading!

Your purchase of this anthology supports the Association of Rhode Island Authors and its mission to raise awareness of the outstanding written works crafted by writers in Rhode Island and in nearby communities. Thank you!

Martha Reynolds

Chair and Editor, ARIA Anthology
Association of Rhode Island Authors

SOMETHING EXTRAORDINARY

A Matter of the Heart

—Jack Nolan

A favorite photo from my childhood, taken in 1952, captures my Aunt Iris, front left, (and insert), then me (age 9) proudly holding aloft the very realistic, two-foot-long rubber rattlesnake Iris gave me, then my mother and angelic sister, beautifully dressed. Like all the other group photos taken by my father with his Kodak Brownie, the people in the back row had to suffer the indignity of decapitation. Over the years, we all learned that if you wanted to be photographed, you sat in the front row.

Like most children, I learned the complex history of my family backwards. On the day immortalized above, I knew only that my favorite aunt liked me, showered me with attention and gifts when she visited, and that she shared with me the feral energy of a child. All other adults were ponderous by comparison. During her visits, she spent more time in our backyard playing ball—any kind of ball—than she did indoors, talking with other adults.

Best of all, if we promised to be good, our mother would let her sister take us home for a week, which meant we packed a suitcase and were driven four hours east on U.S. Route 6 to Iris's house in Bowling Green, Ohio. She lived in heaven, we thought: her enormous "family room" had a television set, a pool table, a ping-pong table, and a fireplace. She taught us how to swim – with great emphasis on "proper form" for the crawl, sidestroke, and backstroke – in her outdoor pool. All this she shared with two floppy-eared cocker spaniels and her partner, Betty. They both taught physical education at Bowling Green University, which made them wealthy by our standards, confirmed when they would hang a bedsheet in the family room and show slides of their trips to the American West, Europe, and Egypt.

Over the years, Iris taught us how to row a canoe, pitch a tent, bait a hook, and clean the fish we caught. And we gradually became conscious of her importance at the university. She had keys to the Olympic-sized natatorium where we two children held sole occupancy until we turned blue with cold and had to come out. We filled a grocery cart with dozens of balls and paddles and rackets and had the run of the college gym, including the full-sized trampoline.

In mid-winter each of those years, our family made a pilgrimage to Bowling Green for the annual "Swan Club" extravaganza. Aunt Iris and Betty coached a synchronized swimming team that put on an eye-dazzling show, filling the natatorium bleachers for four nights. Twenty swimmers costumed with glistening sequins under colored spotlights performed in perfect unison to music that boomed from hidden speakers. One memorable year, my cousin Connie – tall, beautiful, and the object of my first crush – dove off the three-meter board and swam a "shoelace" pattern, crossing the width of the pool from side to side four times to the other end, underwater. When she got to the end, she had been underwater for more than one minute and the entire audience was murmuring and audibly breathing for her. Without surfacing, she kicked off and swam a slow shoelace pattern back again!

My sister and I fell in love with our aunt's world and everything about it, vowing that we would teach in a college someday and live like our aunt did. Even in the limited time we spent with Aunt Iris, strong family bonds were formed between us and secret promises were nurtured about what kind of life we wanted for ourselves.

In 1958, something happened we didn't understand. Iris no longer visited and we received a series of changing and not very convincing excuses from our mother about why arrangements were no longer being made to visit her. Our questions were answered with "Have you taken out the garbage yet?" or "Get the lawn mower out of the garage." The school year was busy, but during long summer days, the phone would ring in the house and we would race over to the screened window to see if it might be Aunt Iris, calling us to the land of our dreams.

In the summer of 1961, family members gathered to celebrate my graduation from high school. One of my father's numerous brothers took me aside to offer me a beer, an initiation to adulthood, I suppose. It tasted like carbonated seawater. Idle talk led to my saying Iris taught me how to swim.

"Oh, yeah," he said, "your mother's butch sister."

I had not the first clue what he had just said. "My mother's what?"

"You knew that, didn't ya? Your aunt was a…like the female version of a fag. She preferred girls to boys, you know. Her girlfriend walked out on her a few years back and that's when we all figured out what the deal was. Your mother hasn't spoken to her since."

Dear reader, you must understand that semi-rural Indiana, a half-century ago, had neither the language nor the understanding to discuss such complex matters, which are not even today completely settled. So please forgive my uncle's crude diction, as well as my own, having only the vaguest notion of what he was talking about. We were both Neanderthals.

However, I did have my own car and enough gumption to phone Iris to ask if I could visit. I was warmly received, with much fuss made over how tall and strong I'd become and how excellent my posture was. "I had no choice," I told her. "You made sure I walked straight, with shoulders back and chin up, when I was a kid."

Over the next two days, I took every opportunity to put a word in about her influence on me and my sister, all that she had taught us, all the ways in which she had shaped our ideas about the professional life. It was very much a "tribute visit" and we both knew it. But not a word was spoken about Betty, her absence from the house, there being one cocker spaniel but not two. It wasn't time yet for a real "adult" conversation, not for me. I didn't know how. I was entering Ball State Teachers College in September, on the Honors Program, and Iris took more glowing pride in that than my own mother did. She had more to do with it, and I made sure she knew it.

On the second night of that visit, the university was hosting a faculty dance, and it was the first time I had ever seen her in a dress, a frilly evening gown. Her date was a gentle little fellow in a tux, who hardly spoke above a whisper. I had ample time that evening, shooting pool in her family room, to reflect on her situation. It was apparent to me, even in my naivete, that Iris and her date were covering for each other – that before "gay pride" was ever uttered, they could lose their hard-won faculty positions and be blackballed from any other teaching job. I got a little choked up in the silent house, thinking about how awful a time my wonderful aunt must have gone through when Betty moved in with someone else. A widow can wail to the heavens when she loses her husband of many years, but Iris had to show the world a calm demeanor and bear the death of that long-time relationship and the embarrassment it caused her in the close-knit faculty community with equanimity. She was even cut off from me, my sister, her sister's family because of whom she loved…then lost.

I made time each summer during my college years for a trip to Bowling Green, where Iris taught me the rudiments of proper form in golf and tennis. During one such visit, she told me she was having open-heart surgery. She showed me an x-ray of her heart, which was enlarged because of a "leaky valve."

"When did you find that out?" I asked.

"I've known about it since I was young. I excelled only in short swimming races and tennis because I run out of breath after a few seconds."

"Good grief! And you chose to major in physical education anyway? Why didn't you have it fixed?"

"They didn't have the means before the mechanical valve came along. After the operation, I'm planning to run a marathon….at 55."

"Right," I said with a laugh. "Well, I've always said you had a big heart, but now I've got proof." Something tugged at me, and I realized how little I knew about her life before she invited me into it. "I don't think I've ever asked where you attended college."

"Western Michigan in Kalamazoo. My sister Winnie and I worked at the Kellogg Institute in the cafeteria and marshalled our resources so I could attend. Without Winnie, I wouldn't have made it through."

In bed that night, I pondered how easy I had it, compared to Iris. I was earning my way through college, sure, but with the help of my dad, who landed me a union job at United States Steel in Gary each summer that paid my way, with enough left over for a car. By the time Iris got to Western Michigan, her father had passed away and she attended classes and served in the cafeteria with a "leaky heart," making it work only because her sister backed her full-time.

I tried to stay in touch whenever a pay phone and enough loose change came together while Iris went through open-heart surgery and a long recovery. After that, I turned my attentions to landing my degree, avoiding the draft at Indiana University grad school and then a teaching deferment while the brief skirmish in Vietnam got wound up. Then it didn't. So, I enlisted in the U.S. Army, served in Vietnam, and came home to a holding company at Fort Meade. Only Christmas cards kept my aunt and me in touch during those years.

I made one last visit to her during my last month of Army service. I was on leave to attend my mother's funeral, then drove east through a blinding snowstorm to that familiar house in Bowling Green. I was expected and Iris put together a delicious dinner while we talked about the family, how everyone had taken my mother's passing. I made sure she knew I was already accepted at Columbia University and how determined I was to earn a Ph.D. and teach college. It was a very sentimental evening, during which she accepted me as the young adult I was, no longer the child she had treated almost as her own years ago.

We sipped through a third, a fourth, a fifth gin-and-tonic before the family room fireplace while the wind drove piles of snow into drifts outside the windows. Iris talked about her father, the grandfather who was never spoken of inside my own family. I learned that he ran away from home at an early age to be a roustabout for a small circus. He was a renowned storyteller with a regular following in taverns he frequented as he moved from job to job. He married, sired Iris and Winnie, then divorced and remarried my grandmother. So, my aunts were half-sisters to my mother. The families were never merged; Iris and Winnie grew up in a state-run orphanage in Danville, Illinois, visited once or twice a year by their father until his death, on an operating table in Gary, Indiana, where ether was overapplied during an emergency appendectomy.

I was twenty-five years old, and all of this was news to me! Why in hell wasn't I ever told about any of this before now?

The next morning, I worked off my well-deserved hangover by digging my car out of the snow. When I returned to the house to warm up, Iris presented me with a thermos of coffee for my trip back to Fort Meade, along with a large glass of water and a pastry. I set everything aside and for the first time in our lives, I put my arms around her. "You are the most remarkable person I have ever known," I whispered in her ear. She answered simply, "Drive carefully. The roads will be icy." But her eyes were glistening.

They are all gone now -- all the aunts and uncles and even the cousins of that generation – and I have tried to make amends by assuring that my own children were told, over time, the story of a woman whose life ran from an orphanage to a respected faculty position and the glory of many Swan Club shows, driving a leaky heart as far as it would go.

Jack Nolan enlisted in Army Intelligence in 1967 and served as a civilian-cover spy, working with Vietnamese counterparts. He forged life-long friendships during that time which are the subjects of his two comic novels – VIETNAM REMIX and THERE COMES A TIME – available upon request at vietnam.remix.1968@gmail.com or on Kindle.

seadevil

— *Stephanie Ann Nary*

Her history is darkness.
Tiny yet fierce.
They fear her.
From the depths
Of the sea,
Of her soul,
She knows
She is meant for more.

Extraordinary.

She makes her own light.
On her back she holds
Him:
An irremovable appendage.
She is his vision.
The perfect host.
Their blood
is one.

Ladened.

She yearns
For light,
For change.
She rises.
The first of her kind.
She is hope.
Unbeknownst to her:
A modern woman.

On February 5th 2025, a deep-sea angler fish was seen swimming near the shore off the coast of Spain. Usually found at depths of between 640 and 6,000 feet, this may be the first ever sighting of the species near the shore in broad daylight.

Stephanie Ann Nary is a dedicated author and school counselor. Her love for literature and her background in counseling combine in her goal to write books that not only entertain but also provide valuable lessons. Her recent book *The Friendship Garden* was featured on The Rhode Show.

Not a Burden

— Sarah P. Blanchard

"What day is it?"

How many times this week has he asked that? How many times today? There's nothing wrong with his hearing. Or his memory.

I stare through green hospital curtains, out the window to a gray March sky. There's nothing there but brick walls and parking lots.

I don't have to turn around right away because I know exactly what the old man on the hospital bed looks like. He is mostly skeleton, so thin now that his elbows poke dents in the mattress. His face is gaunt. There is an ugly stubble on his chin because my mother hasn't had time to shave him.

Only the thick shock of white hair and the pale blue eyes remind me that I've known him in other places and all my life. He's a farmer, though not anymore, and his arms used to be burnt nearly black in the summer sun. He built our stone walls and plowed the fields, first with horses and then with tractors. Now his skin is as pale as the creased sheets he lies on, and nearly as dry. Cancer is turning him to cold pale wax. He is barely here, and soon he will melt entirely away.

"What day?" His voice is sharp and peevish.

"Sunday. It's still Sunday, Daddy." I turn toward him but don't meet his eyes. There's a familiar crack in the wall just over his head. I memorized it weeks ago.

"What *date?*" His voice is hoarse.

"The eighth. March eighth."

He sags back, closing his eyes. I continue to stare at the crack. Beginning at the ceiling, it wanders loosely down the wall, then widens into a deeper channel before feathering into rivulets and disappearing behind the bed. It reminds me of the river that borders our pastures, a strong wide stream where the yearling heifers and wild deer go each day for water.

On the edge of vision I see my father's thin lips move slightly. His tongue pushes out.

I force my feet to carry me to the bedside table where an untouched lunch tray is cooling.

"Are you hungry, Daddy? You haven't eaten. You've got to eat something."

Useless words. He stopped eating a week ago. Only IV tubes feed him now, and he's tried to pull those out.

"No. Maybe tea. Just a little." His voice is whispery, nearly gone after the effort of speaking. He licks his lips without opening his eyes.

A dutiful child, I uncover the little pot of hot water and unwrap a tea bag. I drop it in, careful to hang the string over the edge.

"No. It's too strong. Take it out!" He manages a near-shout and struggles feebly to grab the teabag, knocking over a glass of water on the tray. The bent straw falls to the floor and water runs off the tray.

Annoyed, I stand the glass up and mop tepid water with a napkin. He sinks back into the pillows but his bright pale eyes are still open, watching me. He has no apologies left to give me.

The teabag is still in the pot. I pull it out and pour a half cup of tea.

"Sugar?"

He shakes his head.

"Lemon? Milk?"

He waves a hand and frowns.

I place a straw in the warm, weak tea and hold it so he can drink. He sips a little then closes his lips firmly.

He looks at me but I can't read his eyes. I don't know what he wants to tell me. Whatever it is, I don't want to hear it.

I glance away and immediately flush with shame because there on the counter is the handsome black portable radio his brother gave him. It's the best Panasonic that my uncle's 1964 dollars can buy. My parents have never had the money for such luxuries.

I covet that radio.

What will happen to it when he dies? Will it be mine?

I turn quickly. As punishment for thinking of the radio, I drag the thought of his death forward and try it on. My father will be dead. I will have to explain to people: My father is deceased. My father passed away last week, last month, last year, forty years ago.

I indulge the small child's version of white magic: *Think of the worst, and it will not happen.* When I was little and afraid of the dark, he would hold me in strong arms and coax me to repeat those words. Face your fear, child. Imagine it, confront it, and you can manage it. Bogeymen under the bed, an owl in the pine tree, a looming shape in the closet. Stand it up, drag it out into the light, and demand an explanation.

But that works only with shadows and bedtime stories.

***

My friends at school stopped asking about my father months ago. Except for Charlene. She's not really a friend, just someone in my eighth-grade homeroom.

We could be friends but we're too cautious to make the effort. She's Black, I'm White. She lives down by the railroad yard with a big noisy family; I'm an only child and I live on a dairy farm north of town. A year ago, we read Nancy Drews out loud to each other at recess and this winter we were on the same basketball team, but that's about it. If we'd met when we were little kids we'd probably have become pretty good friends but now it's too hard.

On Friday morning before first period, Charlene dumped her books on her desk and said, "Hey, how's your daddy doing?"

Three other kids near us stopped talking. They looked at Charlene, looked at me, and edged away.

"Not good," I told her. "He's not eating."

The other kids drifted out into the hallway.

"I had an aunt like that," Charlene said matter-of-factly. "After her fella passed on, she just decided to die. They'd lived together nearly forever, I think. 'Don't wanna be a burden,' she told my momma. 'Don't wanna be a burden to my folks.' So she just sorta shut down and died. It was peaceful."

Charlene touched my shoulder, then dropped into her chair. "Of course, she *was* a burden because everyone fussed and tried to get her to eat, but that wasn't her fault. Maybe your daddy's like my Aunt Mabel, just doesn't wanna be a burden."

"Maybe," I said. "But he didn't lose anyone. He doesn't *need* to die. I just wish..."

Charlene tilted her head and waited.

"I just wish he wasn't sick."

What I really meant was, I wish the dying man in the bed wasn't my father. My father had abandoned me. Not all at once in screams and rage and slammed doors, but a tiny bit at a time. He's slicing away the minutes, building walls and slipping off cell by cell while I sleep or listen to music or do my schoolwork. While I'm living my closed-down life.

For every minute that I forget to think of him, I lose a little more of him.

Or maybe what I wanted to say to Charlene was, *I wish I was someone else, somewhere else.* All alone outside this world, galloping a tall horse very fast, riding bareback on a sparkling sand beach. Forever.

★★★

My mother has returned from the ladies' room. She looks old and tired, but I know she is also strong and healthy. She takes in at a glance the wet napkin, the cup of tea, and my awkward, defiant stance. I am back at the window, staring at cars and traffic lights.

I should say something to him about how I love him. Or I should tell him the snow and ice have finally melted into mud in the corn-fields. The sap ran late this year but finally the maples are pushing out those tight red buds that say *Spring.* I should tell him that this morning I saw the first pointed curls of skunk cabbage poking up from the edge of the frog pond. But my voice is stuck somewhere deep, beneath the stone in my chest.

My mother bends over the bed and smiles, murmuring words I can't hear. She smooths his hair back, clucks over the stubble on his chin, and rummages in a drawer for his electric shaver. I smell hospital soap on her hands.

"You'll be going home with Uncle John," she says to me without looking up. "He's in the waiting room. I'm staying here tonight. Say goodbye to your father, now."

Released, I move quickly to my father's side. Hold his hand for a moment and try to keep the relief out of my voice.

"Bye, Daddy. I'm going now."

He closes his eyes and does not speak, but his grip tightens suddenly, painfully. I resist the urge to cry out or pull away. When he finally lets go, I flee down the hall to find Uncle John.

***

We're driving home in the slush and early dusk. The clock on the dashboard of Uncle John's car glows amber and green. His new Lincoln is far finer than anything else I've ever ridden in. My parents drive the farm's pickup or a crumbling Ford that is older than I am.

"You know your dad's dying," Uncle John begins. A statement, not a question.

"Yeah." *Nothing new there,* I'm thinking.

"He loves you. You won't have him with you much longer. You could be a little more understanding." Uncle John must have been talking with my mom.

I want to scream but instead I lean my head against the cool window and try to listen.

My father's brother looks the way my father used to. Solid, square-shouldered, with large hands, a thick shock of gray hair, and a kind face. Uncle John is gentle, soft-spoken and generous, just as my father used to be. He's a banker, though, not a farmer. No sixteen-hour days in the hayfields for him.

I know enough to realize I'm insolent with him because I wish we had his money. Also, he doesn't have cancer and he isn't dying.

I say the first bitter thing that comes into my head. "He'd be okay if he'd just eat. He's given up. He doesn't even *try* to get well." It's his own fault, I mean. He could get better if he really wanted to. If he loved me enough.

"Food tastes pretty awful when you're on those drugs," Uncle John says mildly. "Maybe you wouldn't know about that."

"No, I guess not." I am suddenly very tired. My face is wet from the condensation on the window or something else.

We're both silent for a few minutes. Heading home to a silent empty house, I watch the cold faraway lights of other people's houses swing by. Then we've left behind the lights and the neat tidy houses. We drive through a dark forest where there's nothing but wilderness stretched out beneath the invisible new moon. I imagine white-tailed deer and black bears watching from beneath the oaks. They can see us in the glow of the dashboard but we will never see them.

"You know," Uncle John says quietly, "your daddy wishes he'd been a better father to you."

Caught in self-pity, I straighten up. A slow heat spreads up my neck.

He says, "Farmers don't make much money. I don't have to tell you that. Your dad's a farmer because he loves it. He believes that working the land and loving his family are the most important things anybody can do. But he wishes he could've given you more of the things you want. Clothes, a new TV, your own portable radio."

I think, *Is it that obvious?* Tears threaten but I'm too tough to cry.

Uncle John continues, "He hasn't been able to do much that way. And now his time's up. There's just one more thing he can do to help your mom and you. There's some insurance money. Not a lot, but still something. It's a term policy. You know how that works? If a person dies before a specified date, it pays out. After that date, it expires and isn't worth anything."

Anger lodges in my throat again. *Wow. My dad's dying and my uncle's giving me a lecture on insurance. Go to hell, Uncle John.*

He keeps talking. "That policy expires on the fifteenth. He told me it's like a wall he's got to climb over by that date. Today's the eighth, so he's got seven days. If he lives longer than seven days, there's no money for you and your mom."

He pauses. Adds, "I think he'll make it. Extraordinary, isn't it? What we do for love."

The place I occupy becomes a great hole and I've fallen in. There is no air in the car, no light in the streets. I'm gasping for breath, falling alone through a wilderness of space, clutching a silent black radio to my chest, on the wrong side of whatever boundary is supposed to keep me safe.

Sarah P. Blanchard writes poetry and fiction. Her debut novel, *Drawn from Life*, won a 2025 Independent Press silver medal; two stories were finalists for the 2021 Doris Betts Fiction Award and the 2024 Porch Prize for Short Fiction. She is completing a murder mystery set in northeastern Connecticut. www.sarahpblanchard.com

Mac

— Sam Kafrissen

I have always enjoyed watching baseball. There is something about the easy flow of a baseball game that fits nicely with the soft rhythms of a summer's day. It moves slowly as we all should whenever the temperature exceeds eighty degrees. There is no sense of urgency in a baseball game, nor does it have to adhere to a time clock like most other sports. Baseball sets its own pace based solely on the actions in the game itself. And like life, a baseball game ends only when the final out is made. For me, baseball will always be a game played outdoors in the bright sunshine of a summer's day. This, of course, is seldom the case nowadays with professional games played mostly at night.

I played baseball briefly as a boy but was never very good at it. The hand-eye coordination needed for hitting and fielding just wasn't part of my skill set. I would later gravitate to sports like football and wrestling that valued more macro-type skills. I did play on a Little League team for a couple of years, though I suspect that I was only chosen to be part of the Garden Hardware nine because my older brother Don was the team's star. In our town there were two Little Leagues, an American League and a National League. Each consisted of four teams that oddly never played against one another during the regular season. The teams were sponsored by local businesses and usually bore the name of those enterprises. We were supported by a local hardware store and had no nickname – we were just Garden Hardware. Other teams were the Hornets, the Eagles, the Pioneers, etc. None of the teams in either league bore the moniker of one of the major league teams of the day. There were no Yankees, Red Sox, or Dodgers in our town.

Don was two years older than I and had very quickly acquired some valuable baseball skills after he turned eleven – the most prominent of which was that he could hit for power. That year he knocked out a league-leading seven home runs in the short Little League season to help the Garden squad win the American League championship. He also hit over .600 while playing a very slick-fielding first base. He had one of those giant claw-like first baseman's mitts that would gobble up throws from his fellow infielders. I admired the way he would position himself in anticipation of their pegs with his right foot on the bag and his left stretched out across the baseline. At the last minute he would flick his glove up to stab the tosses from across the diamond. If a throw was low, he would casually dig it out of the dirt with great finesse.

His last year in the league would be my first. I played third base, or at least tried to. I must say I always found it alarming when I took my position to be standing so close to the hitters. Hot caroms smashed my way would often be caught, or rather "knocked down," off my chest, my knees, or that more vulnerable area of the body in between. Unlike Don, I was at best a Punch and Judy hitter who would occasionally rope a single between third and short. More often, however, I would pop up weakly or strike out. I could tell that our manager, Mr. Nash, was disappointed that Don's baseball genes hadn't been passed on to his younger brother. But since my mother was a driver in the team's car pool, I became an accepted, if not vital member of the Garden nine.

When it came to baseball, my mom was another story altogether. To say she was a rabid fan would be an understatement. There were four different Little League fields in our town, including one directly across the street from our house where, ironically, we seldom played. My mother never missed a game and once she had transported a third of our team to the game in her gigantic Mercury station wagon, she would set up her folding aluminum chair and join the other parents on the sideline. Then she would proceed to berate everyone on the field in her loud, cigarette-infused raspy voice. She had no truck with players trying to get on base via a walk, so she would loudly tell a hitter to "take the bat off your shoulder and swing like a man" - a heady message for an eleven- or twelve-year-old boy. If a player tried to steal a base and was thrown out standing up, she'd loudly criticize him for not sliding. Mom was an equal opportunity heckler, so she had no compunction about criticizing players from either team. Batters or pitchers who took too much time getting down to business particularly incensed her.

My mother reserved her most outrageous taunts for the poor umpires, those stout members from the community who had to call every play, including balls and strikes, while parked behind the pitcher's mound. It was not uncommon for her to repeatedly question the quality of their eyesight. One evening she so riled the man in blue that he marched across the field to where she was sitting and insisted that she leave the field lest our team be forced to forfeit the game. At that point, Mr. Nash intervened, and Mom angrily folded her chair and watched the remainder of the game from the front seat of her station wagon.

During these Little League years, news began to circulate around town about a phenomenal player who competed for the DeLuca Hornets in the rival National League. While my brother Don may have been the star of our team, and perhaps even our league, the kid from the Hornets was talked about as if he were the star of all of baseball. His name was Mario Pagano, or Mac as everyone called him. He pitched for the Hornets and when he wasn't pitching, he played shortstop. In those days Little League teams played twice a week, three times at the most if there was a makeup of a rained-out game. However, a pitcher could only pitch once a week. This was a rule instituted to save their young arms from serious injury. I think there may still be such a restriction.

It just so happened that on a day when our team was not scheduled to play, the Hornets, who were sponsored by the DeLuca Nash Rambler dealership, had a game at the field adjacent to our house. It was on that day that I got my first glimpse of the great Pagano. What I saw that evening has stuck with me all these years. Mac Pagano took the mound in his white uniform with purple trim, his purple hat brim perfectly curled. There was nothing physically imposing about him. He was just a touch taller than most of the other players, but no bigger in terms of bulk. In his windup he would bring his two hands up to the tip of his cap, lift his front leg a bit higher than your typical Little League hurler, and then bring a stinging fastball in over the top with such velocity that you could hear the ball pop into the catcher's glove. The batters would either be frozen in their tracks or would swing long after the ball had hit the catcher's mitt.

Although there was a good-sized crowd on hand, I moved around the outskirts of the field throughout the game so I could watch this pitcher hurl from every angle. The Hornets scored two runs in the first and there was never any doubt as to the game's outcome after that. Inning after inning, Mac Pagano poured his sizzling fastball by each opposing hitter, and each quickly went down on strikes. By the fourth inning it dawned on me that no one had even hit a foul ball. When Mac struck out the final batter, word went round the field that he had pitched a perfect game and caused all eighteen batters in the six-inning game to go down on strikes. It was by far the most dominant pitching performance I'd ever seen, even if it was just by a Little Leaguer.

The next time I saw the Hornets play, Mac was not pitching but rather holding down the shortstop slot. There are two things I remember vividly about that game: Mac hit two titanic home runs and in the last inning when an opposing hitter smacked a long fly between the left and centerfielders, Mac backpedaled from his shortstop position to snag the fly before it passed over the fence.

I was now hooked on the Mac Pagano story. Meanwhile, my brother continued to crush the ball as our Garden Hardware squad marched inexorably toward its second straight American League title. In addition to Don, our scrappy catcher, David Nash (the manager's son), provided some additional firepower with his bat, while Jay Houston (was there ever a better baseball name), our pint-sized pitcher, continued to hurl victory after victory. Each week we would wait in anticipation for the delivery of the local newspaper to read Don's press clippings and to check the standings and the stats. He was well on his way to leading our league in batting and home runs and was sure to break his home run record of the previous season. Then I would sneak a glance at the National League stories where Mario Pagano continued to throw no hitter after no hitter. He likewise led his league in batting and home runs but with numbers that were slightly less than Don's totals, much to my brother's satisfaction.

At the end of each season an all-star team made up of the best players from each league would meet to see which squad would go on to statewide, regional, and perhaps even national competition. All these elimination games would culminate at the Little League World

Series in Williamsport, Pennsylvania. First our American League all-stars would have to face the Nationals, where no doubt the great Mac Pagano would be hurling. In addition to Don, Dave Nash, Jay Houston and our shortstop, and later my best friend, Bruce Filler, would represent Garden Hardware in the all-star contest. As always Don brought his trusty bat, Old Betsy, with him for the game. He had named this piece of lumber after Davy Crockett's rifle from the Disney TV series. He'd even used a wood burning set he'd gotten for his birthday to etch the name Betsy into the thick part of the bat. With black tape wound around the handle, it was a formidable looking instrument. Few players used their own bats in those days, as we often just chose a comfortable stick from the bag our manager brought to each practice and game. But Don wanted his own weapon and thought it was Betsy's special powers that brought him such great success.

As expected, Mac Pagano did hurl for the Nationals that day, though he did not set our boys down as easily as he had the other National League teams during the regular season. In his first at-bat, my brother Don struck out after pulling a couple of hard fouls down the left field line. The Nationals scored three runs early off Jay Houston and Mr. Nash was forced to yank his prized hurler in the third inning. A few hits and a costly error later and Pagano had a 5-0 lead and was cruising. In the sixth inning Don came up for what would be his last at-bat in the red pinstripes of Garden Hardware. This time he was not to be denied as he caught hold of one of Pagano's blistering fastballs and drove it deep over the fence in left center field. Don trotted slowly around the bases, clearly savoring the moment. He had knocked out the only home run hit off Mac Pagano in that pitcher's Little League career. It was Don's twelfth home run of the season and as he rounded third, Pagano tipped his hat to my brother. It must have been one of the greatest moments of Don's life.

The National League all-stars advanced to the Rhode Island regional finals, where they won the deciding game on a Mac Pagano one-hitter in which he struck out thirteen of his opponents. They then moved on to the New Englands where they reached the semifinals. Unfortunately, they were eliminated by a team from Swansea, Massachusetts. In that final game Pagano was prevented from pitching though he did hit three home runs in his team's 7-5 loss. Things might have been different for the Nationals if Mac had pitched every game.

The next year, my brother and Mac Pagano teamed up on the Bain Junior High School baseball team. Mac immediately became the school's ace hurler; it took Don an extra year before he could crack the starting lineup. By then other boys had grown bigger and stronger and Don began to morph from the Babe Ruth of Little League fame into a line drive hitter. The fields were bigger and there were no fences, so outfielders could play as deep as they wanted. Home runs were at a premium in this league and Don wisely made the necessary adjustments to become an effective singles and doubles hitter. Pagano still played shortstop when he wasn't pitching, though Coach Frank Tanzi would often put him in right field to save his arm for future pitching assignments. One day the coach summoned Pagano in from right to relieve in the third inning. He had already pitched a one-hitter earlier in the week. On this day he proceeded to give up no hits in his four innings of relief.

I didn't see too many of those junior high contests as I had begun to develop my own athletic and social life. However, I was there one day when the team was facing its archrival from the other side of town, Park View Junior High. It was a hard-fought game that went into extra innings tied 4-4. Pagano was not pitching that day. He did lead off the bottom of the eighth with a double but was stranded on second as the next two batters struck out. Then my brother, batting seventh in the order, cracked a single through the middle of the infield to score Mac and win the game. He was mobbed after the winning run crossed the plate. I ran all the way home to tell my parents about Don's heroics. That night my father took us all out for steak sandwiches at the Jolly Chef to celebrate.

The next year I entered junior high, and Don and Mac Pagano went on to Cranston High School. Mac became a star quarterback on the football team, a high scoring guard on the basketball team, and the ace hurler on the baseball squad. Don continued to play baseball, though his interest in the sport and school in general was waning. He soon discovered girls and hot cars and then got in with what my parents referred to as "the wrong crowd." In terms of baseball, he fully expected to be the starting first baseman his junior year after laboring the previous season on the JV squad. But the team had a big lummox of a kid who could hit the ball a country mile yet couldn't field worth a damn. There was no designated hitter in those days so slow, weak fielding players were often put on first base by default. Much to his disappointment, Don was relegated to right field where mostly he caught mosquito bites. Halfway through the season Don packed up his glove and spikes and quit baseball for good. It was symptomatic of a lot of unhealthy changes he was going through at the time – as by then my parents had more serious concerns about the direction of my brother's life than his baseball career.

I had grown up as a baseball fan, thanks to my mother's interest and to my baseball card collection. Each year we would make one or two trips to Fenway to see the then hapless Red Sox, who featured an aging Ted Williams and little else. I saw Williams hit a couple of prodigious home runs during those years. We even made a few one-day pilgrimages to New York to see the famous Yankee Stadium and the juggernaut that was the Yankees in the 1950s. I saw the great Mickey Mantle, Yogi Berra, Moose Skowron and Whitey Ford. We once drove to Brooklyn to see the Dodgers and the equally famous Ebbets Field. There I watched Jackie Robinson, Duke Snider, Gil Hodges and the portly Roy Campanella cavort. Occasionally when our family went to Philadelphia to visit relatives my great uncle Sid would take my mother and me to Connie Mack Stadium to see the perennially second division Phillies play some National League rival. One time I saw the Cardinals' Stan Musial hit a grand slam home run. I also saw a triple play there but can't recall the details. Suffice it to say as a youth I got to see some of baseball's greats up close and personal, but on a day in, day out basis the greatest baseball player I ever saw was Mac Pagano. Maybe it was because I knew him, as for a while he was a friend of my brother's who occasionally came to our house to shoot hoops and play HORSE with my brother and some other guys in our driveway.

I continued to follow Mac's career at the high school. By his junior year he was one of the most talked about pitchers in the state. That year he racked up seven one-hit games and pitched the team into the state finals where he was outdueled in a 2-1 contest by a kid who had already been drafted by the Milwaukee Braves. The sky appeared to be the limit as Mac entered his senior season. Major League scouts were already flocking to the town stadium where the team played its home games. On Friday nights the games were played under the lights and when Pagano was on the mound the crowds were enormous. You could feel the buzz in the air. But then the worst that could happen did happen. Mac had injured his right shoulder during football season and had not let it heal that winter while he played basketball. By spring he had what they now call a "dead arm." Not only was his senior season in jeopardy, but also any prospects of playing professional ball.

The high school team muddled through the first half of the season at about .500 with Mac playing mostly shortstop or right field. He could still hit better than most of the other players, yet it was his right arm that had brought him glory over the past seven years. By mid-season, however, he began to recover. He pitched a five hitter here, relieved three innings there and little by little regained his old form. Likewise, the team started to win as well.

One Friday night in the middle of the season, Cranston Stadium hosted a high school all-star game to raise money for something called the Athletic Injury Fund. All the best high school players from the Suburban League would face off against those from the Metropolitan League. At the time our high school was part of the Metro League. It was scheduled to be a nine-inning game, and no pitcher could toss more than two innings. The game was a wonderful exhibition of baseball filled with sharp hitting, slick fielding and excellent pitching. The stadium was packed that night and what most of the locals were anticipating was when Mac Pagano would enter the game. As the night marched on there was no sign of our local hero, not even at shortstop. In the bottom of the eighth the Metros jumped ahead 4-3 and word quickly passed through the crowd that Mac had gotten up in the bullpen. In those days the stadium had the kind of bullpens you seldom see outside of the major leagues where the pitchers warm up outside of the crowd's view.

When the Suburbans came up in the ninth for their last whacks Mac Pagano slowly made his way in from the pen. A green warm-up jacket was draped over the right shoulder of his green and gray uniform. The Cranstonites in the crowd stood and cheered wildly.

As he warmed up you could see the snap of the fastball and hear that familiar pop when it hit the catcher's mitt. I can still see him that night as if it was yesterday. The hands going up to the brim of the green cap, the left leg rising into a high kick and then the right arm coming over the top and extending toward the plate. And the ball, well the ball was just a blur as it hurtled toward the catcher. The question on everyone's mind was, "Does he still have it?" After all, he would be facing some of the most formidable hitters in the state. What happened next should go down in Rhode Island sports lore forever. Mac Pagano threw only nine pitches to three batters. All of them were strikes; none of them were even tipped or fouled off. He just blew it by his opponents as if to announce that he was back. When he and his teammates exited the field, the entire crowd stood and gave them a three-minute standing ovation.

Mac was indeed back as he took his turn for the high school nine every other game tossing shutout after shutout. When he wasn't pitching, he was at short and smacking the ball all over the yard. The team made it into the playoffs, easily winning games that Mac pitched and scratching and clawing to victories in ones when he didn't. Eventually the Cranston squad reached the state championship game as they had the year before.

The final that year was held at Deering High School field in West Warwick. It was the town Don and I had grown up in before moving to Cranston and where my brother first played Little League ball. The championship game took place on a cold, windy day, not what you'd expect in early June. My brother and a group of his friends were going to the game, and at the last minute, much to my surprise, he asked me if I wanted to come along. The contest was broadcast on the radio and one of his buddies brought along his transistor radio so we could listen to the commentary as we watched. Mac, of course, would be pitching for the Cranston nine and another highly regarded prospect, Johnny Zielski, would hurl for West Warwick.

Each team put up a single run early on before the game ground into an epic pitchers' duel. With his devastating fastball, Pagano struck out hitter after hitter, while Zielski was mixing speeds enough to keep the Cranston batters off balance all afternoon. The game passed through the high school seventh inning barrier still knotted at one apiece. It remained that way through the major league nine-inning limit. Still both pitchers labored on, seeming to get stronger as the game progressed. When afternoon moved into evening, it turned bitterly cold. Players on either bench hunched together and wrapped their hands in towels to keep them warm. The two pitchers wore hooded sweatshirts under their warm-up jackets while they waited to take the mound again. The game went into the fifteenth inning and was now over four hours long. In Deering's bottom half of the fifteenth their first batter drew a walk. I wondered if Mac was tiring. I was reassured when he struck out the next hitter. The radio commentator announced that this was Pagano's *thirtieth* strikeout of the game, which must, he said, be some kind of record. The next batter hit a hard shot at the third baseman – a made-to-order double play under most circumstances. But it was late in the day and the boy's hands were cold. The ball caromed off his glove into left field and the runner went all the way from first to third. Now more than ever Mac needed strikeout number thirty-one. I crossed my fingers and lowered my head, praying for an out. He got an out all right, on a lazy fly ball to short center. It was just deep enough to entice the runner from third to bolt toward the plate. The Cranston centerfielder made a good throw and it was a close play at the plate but the runner was safe and the game was over. Deering High had won the state title and their supporters went crazy with excitement. Mac Pagano slowly trudged off the field, head bowed in defeat. He had given up three hits all day, had struck out thirty batters over fifteen innings and had lost the most important game of his life on an unearned run.

I never saw Mac Pagano again. That summer he was signed by the Red Sox and sent to their minor league club in Pittsfield, Massachusetts. I tried to follow his minor league career in the *Providence Journal* and *Sporting News*. For a while he pitched well as a reliever but then came up with a sore arm. He kicked around the minors for a few more seasons until his arm just gave out. My mother always said he should have tried to make it as a shortstop instead of a pitcher, and maybe she was right. But I knew once you had commanded the mound as Mac had, it would've been hard to relinquish that domain.

As for my brother, shortly after high school he enlisted in the navy, where he served four years, including a short tour through Vietnam in the early days of that war. As far as I know Don has never played another inning of baseball in his life. At best, he may have played some catch with his son or daughters when they were young.

I still enjoy watching baseball as much as I ever did though I readily admit that I don't know all the players as I once had nor can I remember any of their batting averages. Occasionally these days I'll be taking an evening stroll and come across a Little League game in progress. I'll stop and watch for while, wondering if there's a budding young Mac Pagano among the boys on the field. And if I listen closely enough sometimes, I can hear the faint echo of my mother's voice suggesting that the umpire needs to get fitted with glasses.

Sam Kafrissen is the author of seven Doherty mystery novels, all set in Rhode Island in the late 1950s and early 1960s. In addition, he has had short stories published in three previous ARIA anthologies as well as in short story collections entitled *Mosaic* and *Mosaic 2014*. He has written sports and features stories for local newspapers, the *Arlington Advocate* and the *Provincetown Banner*.

Ellipsis

— A. Keith Carreiro

In the heat of my youth
I would crunch down
onto carpets of madness
with laughter at the foolish
ways of the world.

I strode over the
rugs of reality
while the soles
of my feet felt
the shagged cacklings
of glee glimmer
in the realm of time's
matting:
in tune with the torment
of their inner glimpse
into truth,
into honor, and
into the still brutal
face of hate
and its kisses.

Yet,
like the petals of
the most beautiful flower,
and as the sharpest points
of a mountain range,
the tug of time
leeches my colors
and blurs uniqueness
away from me.

Now —
during the coolness of
my years and
as the covering of
the world unravels before me,
the kingdom of seconds
and the empire of minutes
stride over my life force;

and I? . . .
I toss my laughter away:
a banshee coldly screaming without her magic
a wolf yellowly howling at the moon of death
an angel whitely flaming
into the
silence of heaven

A. Keith Carreiro started writing poetry in high school. Reading, music, storytelling, and movies became some of his major passions, all of which set him on a lifelong path of exploration in creativity. For him, poetry forms the basis upon which all imagination and storytelling unfold.

Aurora Asleep

— William David Curtis

Aurora Rose wouldn't wake up. She wasn't dead; that much was certain. Her frantic parents had rushed her to the hospital where she was expertly examined by numerous specialists, all of whom testified that she was very much alive. Her doctors knew only what her ailment *was not*: not coma, not narcolepsy, not idiopathic hypersomnia. They did *not* know what it *was*.

One young resident who had taken a special interest in Aurora's case observed something the others had failed to notice. On the side of Aurora's left thumb was a tiny drop of dried blood as though made by a pinprick. He contacted her family to inquire if they knew how she might have received the injury. At first, her parents had no idea, but then Aurora's father, Felix Rose, recalled that the morning of the day she fell asleep, Aurora had been working at the university lab where she was pursuing a doctorate in biochemistry. Felix immediately phoned her doctoral advisor, Benjamin Miller.

"Aurora was studying how bears and other mammals hibernate," Dr. Miller explained. "She was trying to develop something like a sleeping potion that would work for humans. Her hope was that it could be used to conserve energy for interstellar space travel."

Dr. Miller had devoted most of his life to academia and loved nothing more than to share his knowledge. "The scientific name is torpor. It is astonishing what hibernating bears do. Their metabolism is reduced by half; their heart rate slows from forty beats per minute to eight beats per minute and their body temperature drops by three to seven degrees Celsius. They don't eat or drink and they rarely urinate or defecate. They have this unique ability to recycle their—"

Felix interrupted. "Is it possible that Aurora succeeded, that she may have discovered this hibernation serum and accidentally pricked herself on a hypodermic needle when she was testing on a rodent?"

"It certainly is possible," replied Dr. Miller. He struggled to find something reassuring to say. "You know," he continued, "there are documented cases of people surviving exceptionally cold temperatures by falling asleep as a means to reduce their metabolism."

Aurora's father turned hopeful. "Dr. Miller, do you think it might be possible to come up with an antidote? If not, Aurora may never wake up."

"Yes, I agree. She may sleep until the effects of the serum wear off, and that could be years." Dr. Miller endeavored to be optimistic. "I can't say for certain but we can try. Our lab technician has all of her notes and results of her tests. Aurora supervised graduate students working with her on the hibernation project, and they may be able to fill in the details." As an afterthought, Dr. Miller added, "Your daughter shows great promise."

For the next several weeks, Aurora's colleagues worked feverishly to the point of exhaustion in order to develop an antidote to the hibernation serum. Dr. Miller expedited approval for the team to perform tests on groundhogs, squirrels, and other small hibernating mammals. They grew more confident with every subsequent test, adding new compounds, eliminating formula constituents that had disappointed, and retaining others that showed promise. At last, the team believed they had a final product that might reverse the effects of the hibernation serum.

The potential antidote was cautiously transferred to a glass vial, padded in wads of cotton, and rushed to the top floor of the hospital where Aurora Rose remained in a dormant state.

Coincidentally, the same young resident who had first noticed the pinprick, and whose name happened to be Alistair Prince, was on duty. As Aurora's father Felix anxiously looked on, Alistair injected a few drops of the antidote into the IV that kept the unconscious patient supplied with nutrients.

Initially, nothing happened. For several seconds, there was no change to Aurora's breathing. But then, faint signs of movement were visible, suggesting to Alistair the dawn sunlight gradually overcoming the darkness of night. Aurora's eyelids flickered slightly and a neck muscle appeared to twitch. Almost imperceptibly but undeniably, Aurora began to awaken. At long last, after what seemed like an eternity, Aurora's eyes opened fully and she gave a quiet yawn.

"Where am I?" she asked.

"You're in the hospital," Alistair answered. "What is the last thing you remember?"

"Let's see. I was in the lab extracting blood from a hamster in preclinical trial. I thought she was fully sedated, but she suddenly squirmed, and I think I pricked my finger. I wanted to observe the protocol, but I got so sleepy. I tried hard to stay awake but..." Her voice trailed off. "And that's the last thing I remember. How long have I been asleep?"

"Almost eight months."

"Eight months? Really?"

Alistair could not suppress his curiosity. "I have to ask this. The monitor showed you were in REM sleep for an inordinate time. Were you dreaming a lot?"

"Yes, I dreamt a lot. I had so many dreams I can't remember them all," Aurora replied, stifling another yawn. "The last dream I remember was that you and I were getting married on the campus. Isn't that peculiar? I never even met you before now."

Alistair responded with silence. What he remembered was how lovely Aurora appeared peacefully asleep, her long golden hair spilling over her luminous skin, and now, how angelic she looked, her green eyes flashing him an incandescent smile.

One year later in early spring, when hibernating bears were just beginning to emerge from their winter dens, Drs. Aurora Rose and Alistair Prince were married on the beautiful university campus, surrounded by Aurora's adoring family, loving friends, and admiring colleagues. Aurora sold the rights to the hibernation serum—and the antidote—to a pharmaceutical company which, in turn, sold it to the space agency for a healthy sum. Still conscious, Aurora gave birth to twins, and with her generous portion of the serum sale, the newlyweds bought a home in Hawaii where the temperature never gets cold enough for metabolism to halve.

William David Curtis is a member of the Society of Children's Book Writers and Illustrators (SCBWI). His picture books include *The Penguin Who Wanted to Fly,* which one reviewer called "a stunning piece of writing with a tender but powerful tone." He is a contributor to the bimonthly, *Magazine A Praça* (Town Square). William is currently at work on a musical adaptation of a television play, *The Genie of Sutton Place.*

Dubois, Wyoming 1969

— *Robert Bailey Stone*

South of Yellowstone National Park is the very small town of Dubois (pronounced DEW-boyz), Wyoming. It is surrounded by three mountain ranges: the Big Horn, Wind River, and Washita Mountains. In June 1969, I came to this town to attend a six-week field camp required for my B.S. degree in Geology. Prior to that, the farthest west I had been was probably West Orange, New Jersey.

When I found out I was required to attend a geology field camp, it was late in the year for registering for summer camp. Most camps were already filled. I did find two camps still accepting applications, one in Mississippi and one in Wyoming through Miami University of Ohio. When I discovered there were no alligators or poisonous snakes at elevations over 7,000 feet, the camp in Wyoming immediately won out.

I received a list of people who would be attending the camp from the New York area. I contacted one guy named Jeff and asked if he would like to drive cross country with me. He expressed interest in seeing some of the same sites I wanted to see as we drove west. Also, Jim Wasmund was a friend from college who had expressed an interest in driving cross country. Jeff and I would pick him up at his home outside of Buffalo, New York.

Jeff met me in Schenectady, New York, and we took off the second weekend of May in my 1962 Ford Galaxy 500 convertible heading to the Buffalo area where Jim would join us. We headed west and picked up Jim. We were ready to leave early the next morning. Having driven the entire day and into the night, we neared Chicago in the early morning hours of the next day. With darkness still upon us, we decided to detour through the city on a toll road called the Chicago Skyway.

One of the items I had somehow acquired during my college years was a yellow construction flasher. I took this with us just in case we had car trouble on the road. We decided, as a lark, to stick it in the crack between the two front seat backs, and with the top down, we turned on the yellow flasher and headed down the Chicago Skyway.

As we approached the first set of toll booths, we saw one of the gates open. An individual came out of the booth and waved us through without having us stop to pay the toll. This same scenario repeated itself at every toll plaza. We were stunned. We drove through the city of Chicago in forty-five minutes on the Chicago Skyway, paying not one toll!

We crossed the Mississippi River at Davenport, Iowa and stopped for breakfast. So far, I had driven from Schenectady to Davenport. I was beat. I'm not sure who took over driving, but I got in the back seat and slept for about eight hours. When I awoke, we were still in Iowa. Nothing but corn as far as I could see. Just corn.

When we finally reached the western border of Iowa, we turned north to South Dakota, then headed west into Wyoming. We drove through the Badlands National Park, getting lost for a few miles. We stopped at the Mount Rushmore Monument and the Crazy Horse Monument that had only recently been started. We made a detour just over the border into Montana to see Devil's Tower. As geologists, we were interested in seeing this volcanic plug with its vertical fractures the size of railroad boxcars.

When we had crossed a fair amount of Wyoming, the sun had set, and we were on a state route with little traffic. We kept noticing that the stars would periodically seem to disappear from over us and the road kept climbing through twists and turns, and our headlights would occasionally cast their beams into nothingness. Finally, we reached a small town named Ten Sleep, Wyoming. We were exhausted and hungry, having not eaten since breakfast. We stopped at what looked like a small motel with a sign out saying "Vacancies." The place was more of a car park of the 1930s: a home with an office and three or four cabins for nightly rentals.

We asked our host where we might find something to eat. She stepped out the door and pointed to some lights to the north.

"That's the interstate," she stated. "They're always open."

So, even though it was late, we decided we needed to eat. We needed gas, as well. An hour later, the lights appeared to be getting no closer and our gas gauge was getting even lower. Another half hour and we rolled into the interstate truck stop on fumes. We filled our gas tank and our bellies as well, and realized we now had to make the return trip to Ten Sleep since we had left our gear in our room.

The next morning, we decided to retrace the road on which we had arrived in Ten Sleep just to see what we had missed in the darkness. It was frightening. We had come through a pass in the front range of the Rockies and there were no guardrails on those hairpin turns we had traveled. The pass we had come through was not the South Pass we had intended to use, but a much smaller and much steeper pass not used by commercial traffic. Had we been able to see what we were driving in daylight, we would have crawled down the route.

We stopped at several lesser-known landmarks before reaching Cody, Wyoming and the eastern entrance to Yellowstone National Park. It was in Cody that we decided to lose some of our eastern dress and become a bit western. Each of us left town sporting a new western-style hat and shirt that made us feel we "fit in" better with the locals.

The eastern entrance to Yellowstone National Park was only a few miles west of Cody and we were greeted at the entrance by an enthusiastic Park Ranger who informed us that we would probably not see much of the park's wildlife since most of the herds would already be grazing in the high meadows. It had been an early spring, and they were free of snow. He would never know how wrong his prediction was.

We spent a day and a half in Yellowstone seeing elk and moose frequently. We had been told that if we should encounter bears to slow down, stay in our car, and keep the windows rolled up. Sure enough, the bears were out on the road looking for food and, as instructed, we closed our windows. We did forget the convertible top was down and a standing bear is easily taller than the side of a car.

A chance encounter with a buffalo at the mud pots almost led to disaster. I had just loaded film in my Pentax camera as I started down the wooden walkway leaving the mud pots, with Jim and Jeff trailing behind me. As I came around a bend, there in front of me stood a huge bison not four feet away. His massive shoulders were even with my eyes and his horns about the level of my groin. I froze. As my companions caught up with me, they were in animated discussion. I tried to shoosh them softly so as not to frighten the large wild animal before me. I could not move, not even to snap a picture. His head was enormous, and his eyes held a malevolent stare. After a moment, my two friends standing behind me stopped talking and said, "Oh, it's just a statue." At that point, the "statue" swooshed his tail to brush away a fly, and my two friends took off left and right, climbing the nearest trees they could find, leaving me to face the bison alone. Fortunately, their action must have confused the bison, and he wandered off onto the mud for a good roll.

In 1969, Dubois, Wyoming, consisted of only a few stores lining the main route through the town. The main street was a state-numbered route that was unpaved. The main businesses of the town consisted of three saloons (yes, saloons), two mercantile stores, a diner, a gas station, and a jail carved into one of the mountainsides. It felt like I had stepped back into the late 1870s.

That feeling was only further confirmed after visiting one of the mercantile establishments. It was like stepping back into one of those early photographs of the old west. After wandering through the store in near disbelief, I purchased a one-pound slab of beef jerky as had been recommended in my camp informational materials. Since I knew the class was "in the field," I knew I could slice off edible pieces with my knife and the remaining chunk could be wrapped and easily carried. Unlike the packaged jerky sold back home, this was the real thing: impervious to any form of spoilage or contamination but required time to rehydrate and soften in the mouth and make it edible.

Since it was late in the day, the three of us decided to see if the saloons of Dubois were anything like the appearance of the mercantile we had just visited. We entered one of the three in town and stepped up to the bar that ran along the side wall of the building. The bar was bustling with customers. My first observation as I looked up and down the bar at those sipping their various beers and drinks was that my group were the only people at the bar not wearing a holstered sidearm. It was a revelation.

As I stood there surveying the room and feeling again that I had time-warped to the Old West, I noticed an old-style wooden telephone booth in an alcove against the far wall. I had recently become engaged to my future wife, and I decided to call her and tell her I had arrived safely in Wyoming. This was 1969; cell phones were yet to be invented and the internet was unknown. I confidently strolled to the booth and threw open the door. Imagine my surprise when the light came on and I saw no phone! Instead, sitting in the booth was an elderly bearded man who could have passed for a grizzly mountain man of the 1870s. He was dressed in buckskin with a fur cap, had a small fox sitting on his shoulder, and a glass of beer on a shelf where the phone should have been. He was as surprised as I, from his expression. I apologized for disturbing him and quickly stepped back.

Coming back to the bar, I asked the bartender if there was an actual pay phone somewhere I could use. He pointed to the door and directed me to a pole on the street holding the only pay phone in town. As I lifted the receiver and dialed the operator to make a collect call to my fiancée, snowflakes began falling. Welcome to early June in the mountains of Dubois, Wyoming.

That night we stayed in Riverton where there was an airport farther south on the same road, and we put my friend Jim on a plane early the next morning. Jeff and I drove back to begin our six weeks of a rustic western experience. The base camp for the course was the Welles family ranch just a little north of Dubois. The landmark for finding the lane to the ranch was the KOA (Kampgrounds of America) sign beside the entrance. Little did I know this KOA would be an important refuge for the next six weeks. The main house of the ranch was set back a few hundred yards from the highway and there were several outbuildings or bunkhouses and a barn beyond. Mr. and Mrs. Welles were cattle ranchers who had hosted Miami University's summer geology field camp for several years. They had three sons who occupied one of the bunkhouses. More about them later.

Our group consisted of fifty students, fifteen girls and thirty-five guys from all over the United States. We had three instructors and a couple of local guides we called "cowboys." At our first session, our professors explained that we would be traveling on horseback through the surrounding mountains, carrying out mapping exercises, stratigraphic studies, and doing geological profiling. We would leave each week at sunrise on Monday morning and return sometime on Saturday late in the afternoon to our base camp, the Welles ranch. Tomorrow, Sunday, would be spent selecting our mounts which we would have for the next six weeks.

The next morning, we all assembled at the corral, some of the group still frightened at the thought of riding a horse. I had some experience riding as a kid. It had been the usual urban experience: arrive at the barn, the horse is saddled and ready to go, you get on and ride the bridle path around the circuit, and come back to the barn, dismount, and hand the horse off to someone else who would take care of unsaddling, etc. I discovered this was not going to be that kind of sanitized experience. Some in our group had never sat a horse and were terrified by the actual size of these beasts. It was late in the day when each of us finally had our four-legged transports for our journey and received instructions on how each of us would be responsible for the care and feeding of them, to the saddling every morning and hobbling of them at night for the next six weeks.

At sunrise Monday morning, we were all in our saddles waiting for instructions. We were introduced to our chuckwagon and our chef-of-sorts, "Cookie" by name, who would be providing our meals in the field. And so, with some of us still having considerable hesitation, we headed out into the mountains for five days of who-knew-what, but, excitement, nevertheless.

That first Monday was only a gentle example of what was to come. The scenery was magnificent. As we rode up the ridges of the Wind River Range, the clean air and light winds were exhilarating. But as the hours passed, the heat of the day continually increased and became oppressive, and water was a sought-after commodity, especially for those who forgot their canteens. We crested a ridge in the trail and saw below us a small body of water. Our guide informed us we were seeing Mosquito Gulch.

Many of us laughed at such a quaint western name. But as we approached to quench our thirsts, it seemed like the whole top layer of the water lifted off in one gigantic mass of dark-winged insects. Mosquito Gulch was aptly named. Regardless, our group quickly scrambled down to the water to drink when our guide bellowed in a perfect western twang, "Yer horse drinks first. He's yer 'transpertation.'"

One member of our group cleverly responded, "Well, I'm down here and he's up there. How am I supposed to give him water?" The reply came from our guide: "You got a hat, don't cha?" My beautiful, new, formed-felt cowboy hat, recently purchased in Cody, became the vessel for carrying water to said steed, who slobbered in it gratefully at my offering. After his thirst was eased, my now-deformed hat was plopped back on my head. Lesson learned.

That first day turned out to be the easiest of the next six weeks. We rendezvoused with Cookie and the chuckwagon as the sun began dropping behind the hills in the west and shared a wonderful first meal around a campfire. Sleeping under the stars was the most amazing experience. For the first time in my life, I saw the Milky Way in all its magnificence far from any city lights. Now I understood what was meant by majesty.

Next morning, I tried shaving in the mountain stream that flowed near our temporary camp. The stream was fed from a glacier higher up in the mountains and was freezing. I immediately decided I was going to grow a beard for the duration. Breakfast was a new experience. The flapjacks and bacon were the best ever, but the coffee was another lesson. Our coffee was what was referred to as "range coffee." The large coffee pot was filled with cold water, grounds were added, and the pot was put directly on the fire grate. Once the pot boiled, it was set to the side to allow the grounds to settle out. It was best to be someone who got an early cup of coffee after the settling. Otherwise, you'd be chewing as well as drinking your coffee.

Every day in the field was a new experience. We moved early each morning and met up with the chuckwagon sometimes for lunch and always for dinner. We rode along trails we did not recognize as trails. We descended into canyons and climbed ridges to see formations and map stratigraphy. We saw country that no tourist would ever see unless they were on horseback.

After six days in the heat and dirt of the field, there is nothing pretty about a woman or handsome about a man. As we headed back to base camp on Saturday in the afternoon, all any of us could think about was a warm shower and our waiting bunks. Little did we know what awaited us. Before we could enjoy that dreamed-of shower, we had to take care of our horses: unsaddle and water them down and feed them. Then a mad dash to the bunkhouse.

What none of us knew that first Saturday was the limited hot water that was available for a shower. Shower water was heated by the sun beating down on the tin roof of the water tank by each of the bunkhouses. With fifteen of us in each bunkhouse, if you were not one of the first three or four to shower, your shower was ice cold.

Dinner was in the main house with setup and cleanup done by our group. A short meeting was held to talk about what we had done the past week and our time to meet on Sunday to get our assignments for the following week. Then we were free. The KOA bar became the destination for many of the group.

It's only natural in a group such as this that friendships develop quickly with some. In my case, it was a guy from Ann Arbor, Michigan, by the name of Larry Bailey. Larry was a grad student I believe from the University of Michigan, a little older than me and a little shorter. For those who are old enough to remember 1969, Ann Arbor was being terrorized that spring by a strangler, who was loose in the city. Larry worried about his fiancée's safety and was constantly trying to call her. Being newly engaged was something we had in common.

We began working as a team in the field in the weeks ahead. Our weather continued hot and sunny with heavy morning fog and dew. As we worked at mapping strata and fault lines in the hot sun, we naturally wanted to strip off our overshirts. This, we discovered, was a bad mistake. At 7,000 feet and higher, the sun burns skin quickly. A few members of the group made the same mistake as I did, and we all suffered second degree sun poisoning. Fortunately, it was on Saturday before heading back to base camp and those cold showers would suddenly feel extremely good on our backs. Unfortunately, it also caused the skin to blister and peel, and the more tender skin beneath to weep; another painful lesson learned.

For the remaining four weeks of field camp, I, along with my fellow sunburn victims, were very cautious about uncovering in the field. But the magnificent landscapes we experienced made up for the discomfort we felt. We learned the history of the Wind River, Washita, and Big Horn mountain ranges, both geologic and historic. We saw the remains of sluiceway tunnels cut through canyon walls during the time when logging was a major industry in those hills. We saw elk and bison, jackrabbits, and pronghorns. We witnessed magnificent sunrises and sunsets that were beautiful beyond description. And through it all, we rode our horses.

The nights were cool, but not cold. Sleep was easy unless you were chosen for guard duty. Yes, we had to take turns guarding our temporary camps each night. Sleep was peaceful, until someone dropped a thirty-thirty rifle in your lap and informed you it was your turn at guard duty. It was a wonder none of us ever had to shoot it.

One Saturday evening before heading to dinner, we were surprised to hear sporadic gunfire. Curiosity brought us to the bunkhouse occupied by the Welles's sons. In Wyoming in 1969, there were small ground squirrels called picket pens. That was the name we were given for these animals. On our drive out of Yellowstone, we observed the creature. They would run out into the road in front of cars and stand erect, attaining a height of about a foot. A loud 'thud' would be heard as they were hit by the car bumper. Hitting the brake in a moment of terror and screeching to a stop, if you looked in the rearview mirror, you would see them tumbling down the road. They would then spread their legs and run off to the side of the road, uninjured. We were told they did this with cars 'for fun.'

One evening, we watched the Welles's sons sitting outside their bunkhouse drinking beer and shooting at picket pens as they scurried about from burrow to burrow in the field outside their cabin. Such was entertainment on the Welles ranch in 1969.

On the last day of our work in the field, we arrived at the Welles ranch looking very different than when we left on that first morning six weeks earlier. Our clothes were not neat and clean. We all sat in the saddle a little more comfortably, and we looked less like city folk just attending a dude ranch.

To celebrate the successful conclusion to our stay, Mr. Welles took a group of us down to one of the pastures and told one of the girls to pick out a steer, which she did. He promptly shot it, and his sons butchered it. After helping the girl recover from the shock of her fatal choice, we watched as the Welles boys built a fire pit and hung a hind quarter over it on a spit. A few hours later, we all enjoyed a real Western-style barbecue. Anyone who says meat needs to be aged has never had beef off the range. It was the best I have ever tasted.

When our course work final exam was taken and it was time to leave, there was a certain sadness that settled over the group. As anxious as everyone was to return home, it was the loss of those short friendships, formed from a common experience, that brought some tears, knowing we would never all be together again.

I was in a hurry to get back to New York and my fiancée, so I cut quite a swathe across the Midwest. I drove back across the country alone as Jeff had decided to fly home. I was stopped for speeding outside Cheyenne, Wyoming, Lincoln, Nebraska, and Council Bluffs, Iowa. It was in Iowa that the officer informed me that all the states I had traveled through in the past twenty-four hours were all connected electronically, and I was blazing quite a trail for myself. Fortunately, every one of these fine law officers saw fit to let me off with a warning. I finally crashed in a motel in Geneseo, Illinois, and slept for about eight hours. When I reached North Tarrytown, New York, I slept for a solid twelve hours. After waking, I happily shaved my six-week beard and took a long, hot shower. I looked out the window at my car parked on the street and discovered every possible fluid it contained was leaking out onto the street. My car was officially deceased.

By 2005, I had been married for thirty-five years. I had always delighted in telling stories of my Wyoming experience, so much so that my wife wanted to see for herself the locations for these wild tales. Since she had never traveled west, we decided to trace my 1969 route to Wyoming. So, we headed out across America.

We had little interest in seeing anything east of the Mississippi River other than Chicago. So, once across the Mississippi, we crossed Iowa, turned north at its western border to Sioux Falls, South Dakota. From there we headed west again, going through the Badlands, stopping at Mount Rushmore (terribly commercialized since my last visit), the Crazy Horse Monument (some progress made since 1969), and Devil's Tower.

We continued across Wyoming to the city of Cody and entered Yellowstone National Park through its east gate just as I had done thirty-six years before. Yellowstone in early October is beautiful. We spent an entire day touring the park. We saw bears and had an encounter with a bull elk. No one told us that the harem of female elks that passed in front of our car would be followed by the male. He was ready to charge our car for getting between him and his harem. We got in the middle of a herd of buffalo so close to the car, my wife could reach out the car window and pat one on the rump. We drove 350 miles and never left the park. We had reservations at the Old Faithful Inn. It was closing for the winter the next day and we awoke to several inches of new-fallen snow.

After our day and a half in the park, we left by the south entrance and drove south on the highway that was now paved. We stopped to admire the Grand Tetons which were originally named by a French explorer as "Grande Tetons," meaning great breasts. He must have been alone for some time since there are three peaks not two.

After a little more driving, I found the Welles Ranch. The landmark of the KOA was now a heavy equipment dealer. At the entrance to the ranch was a sign declaring the facility was now the summer geology camp of Miami University of Ohio and was owned by them. As far as I could tell, the buildings looked the same from a distance. I was disappointed at not being able to introduce my wife to the Welles family.

Once we had gotten to the former Welles Ranch, the tracing of my 1969 journey was completed. From there, we continued west to California where both our sons were living. Our trip back east is a tale for another time.

Robert Bailey Stone has had two books published: *The Chronicles of Benjamin Prescott*, a novel of historical fiction and *Murder in Rock Cove*, a murder/mystery. Mr. Stone became a writer after a career in insurance and financial planning. His stories originate from dreams.

Ollie

— *Eric Crook*

During the early days and months of COVID we did our fair share of worrying, handwringing, and becoming thoroughly despondent. We recoiled in abject horror, as pundits prognosticated viral apocalypse, and our addled president reassured the public by shooting as many messengers as he could shake a stick at.

We watched the horrifying news and took to reading as an escape from reality. In quest of a modicum of intellectual betterment in the days we had left before the coronavirus dispatched us all to the pearly gates, I started reading the classics. You know what I mean, all those revered tomes that everyone swears up and down they know like the backs of their hands every time they are mentioned. I'm referring to Theodore Dreiser, Dickins, Joyce, Chekov, Marquez, and of course, Samuel Clemens.

My favorite reading spot was, and still is, our green leather couch in the TV room, with the backyard out my window and the sliding glass door looking out on the deck over my right shoulder. That day I was reading Mark Twain. As best as I can recall it was *A Connecticut Yankee in King Arthur's Court* when, out of the corner of my eye, I spied an incredible flash of colors, mostly orange, zooming past the window, alighting ever so briefly on the bird feeder hanging below the veranda, only to streak away into the blue morning sky.

I had heard recently that there were Oriole sightings in the neighborhood, but this was the first time I had ever seen one in my yard. I will readily admit that I took a course in Ornithology in college. Why? Who does that? I have never been certain why I did. My mother and I used to attract birds with suet and sunflower seeds when I was a kid. Once a brave, or more likely, short-sighted, black-capped chickadee took a seed from my palm. Maybe that was when I got hooked.

But under the burden of isolation that moment took on a far greater meaning. It became my *raison d'être*. We learned that Baltimore Orioles were particularly fond of Welch's grape jelly. So I didn't wait for delivery, I donned a mask (N-95s were not yet commonly available), drove to the supermarket, bought a two-pack of 32-ounce plastic jars of grape jelly, and then I picked up a red, cup-shaped, hanging feeder that was recommended to me by my friends at Wild Birds Unlimited.

By noontime, the stage was set. I loaded the feeder with grape jelly and waited. It didn't take long for Ollie to show up, check out the new feeder, grab three bites of jelly and scram. A minute passed. He returned, brilliant orange, contrasted with a jet-black head and mantle, while bright white coverts emblazoned his wings, like a lieutenant in full parade dress. I have seen the Roseate Spoonbills of Florida, the Blue-headed Macaws, and the Green Parakeets. I've even seen the Elegant Trogon that never strays farther north than southern Arizona, and yes, I once had a rare sighting of a Wilson's Phalarope brought in by a storm on the Puget Sound. But having an Oriole living in my own backyard - that was something special.

There is nothing more captivating than an Oriole in flight, darting fast and self-certain through the air and from branch to branch. I could draw trite comparisons to Brooks Robinson and the great Oriole teams of the late 60s, but no, Ollie deserves better. The Baltimore Oriole is a fierce defender of its turf and Ollie is no slouch, dropping a wing to turn on a dime and warn off a Blue Jay or noisome Grackle.

He's more like the British Spitfire that regularly outmaneuvered the much larger Messerschmitt during the Battle of Britain. Little wonder that, with the entire bird kingdom to choose from, *The Sibley Field Guide to Birds* has an Oriole in flight adorning its front cover. During numerous flybys, Ollie gorged on grape jelly all afternoon. He came back the next day, and then most every day after that. Always watchful, carefully appraising the situation before he would swoop in and start gobbling down the jelly.

A month or so into his second year with us he brought home a girlfriend – Olivia. She had the characteristic markings of the female: the head was not black, but brownish-yellow and her body was orange-yellow. Like most species in the avian domain, the colors of the female *Icterus galbula* are muted in comparison to the male. He would eat first and she came second while he stood guard. Needless to say, she quickly earned our approval. Thus, it was in mid-July when their child, Ophelia, made her first appearance.

For the life of me, I cannot say that the more extraordinary thing was that this beautiful family graced our home for all those days. Or is it that Ollie, Olivia, and little fledgling Ophelia took the edge off those brutal days of COVID and brought earnest hope to my state of mind. So it remained, until late summer, when it was time for Ollie and his family to begin that long trek to Florida, the Caribbean, Central America, and worlds unknown. But that was only the beginning. My Orioles have returned every spring since, and last year they surprised us again with a son. Oppenheimer, and he is destined to be an award winner for years to come.

Eric Crook is a regular contributor to the ARIA anthology and is a member of the ARIA Board. His first novel, *Between a Rock . . .* debuts this spring with Gatekeeper Press. He has two sequels in the works, altogether comprising the Gansted Trilogy. Though originally from New York, he now lives in Rhode Island.

George and Tony

— Rick Billings

Among my mementos I have an old, faded picture of myself taken
by my mother. I'm standing in our kitchen at the apartment on
Jefferson Avenue. Sporting what looks like a fresh haircut, a bowtie,
and my ever-present red blazer, I am smiling. Sitting next to me is
our dog Flippy. Flippy was pure mongrel. "A Heinz!" as my dad used
to say with a chuckle - like he'd just made it up. "57 Varieties!" Flippy
was a small black dog with a white chevron on his chest and a red
collar. A quiet, gentle fellow.

Most photos in the early sixties had the date of development im-
printed on the border. The date on that one read "Jul 65" making me
around six years old when it was taken. When I see that smiling boy
looking back at me, I see the innocence and purity of youth. I think
about all the events and challenges ahead in his life. But at that moment, it was just a boy and his dog.

My mom loved animals, especially dogs and cats. She realized the
comfort and value that pets have for children. There were other animals before Flippy of course, but he is the first that I was aware of. It
just seems that he was always there.

I'm not sure how old I was when it happened, but I do remember
my mom telling me that Flippy was sick. She may have told me that
he was going to heaven or to a "farm" or just to sleep. I did understand

that he wasn't coming back. I may have been sad or upset. I'm really not sure. I was too young to have any real grasp of it. One day Flippy was there, the next he was gone.

Within a few days, Mom asked me if I wanted to go with her to the pound and get a new dog. Excited like anyone that age about the prospect of a puppy, I eagerly agreed. Early on a Saturday morning, we drove to Providence to the Animal Rescue League. In the mid-1960s the standards for animal care and wellbeing were not what they are now. I wasn't fully prepared for the chaos that greeted us as we were led into the outdoor holding area. It was a large enclosure with what seemed like hundreds of dogs. They all came charging to the fence when we came out. There was frantic barking and yelping - each one seeming to say "Pick me! Take me home!"

There were so many dogs crammed into a little space that it was difficult to get a look at just one.

Between the outdoor holding pens there were large metal plates hanging on the fence, presumably to keep the more aggressive dogs from lunging at dogs on the other side. Caught behind one of the plates was a small brown and black puppy struggling to get out to join the "Pick me!" chorus. I immediately felt bad for the dog. It wouldn't take a genius therapist to make the connection — even at that age I'd often felt caught behind the metal plate myself. I didn't hesitate and told my mom, "I want that one." For years she would tell this story, proudly citing my concern and compassion for the trapped dog.

We spent some time sitting in a cold office while Mom filled out forms taking ownership of the puppy, promising to get it licensed and spayed. She paid whatever fee was required, counting out the bills one at a time. The man behind the desk informed us that our new dog was a female and that her name was Phineas Good Nature. Thus began our long adventure with "Phinny."

As I mentioned, my mom loved animals. She felt that a home (and a boy) should have a dog. It didn't matter that she was juggling three daughters of various ages and a young son. It didn't matter that my dad was in absentia most of the time. And it didn't matter that our family at that time was ill-equipped to raise and properly care for a new puppy. Whatever our economic situation, we always had a dog.

Phinny made her presence known from the start. She was a headstrong, difficult dog who did not live up to her full name. I had no idea how to train a dog or to teach it not to pee and poop in the house. Mom didn't have the time. My sisters, other than being disgusted by it, were seemingly indifferent to the issue. As a result, we would regularly deal with cleaning up Phinny's accidents throughout the house, but mainly on the floor under the kitchen table. If my dad had been home more, he not only could have helped train the dog but could have schooled me in correcting her behaviors. My grandfather, his dad, raised and trained beagles for hunting and for show. Visiting my grandparents in Attleboro was always a thrill for me because Grandpa let me go out to the kennel and see the dogs. I was usually more interested in doing that than playing with any of my cousins who were there. The kennel was a cold, cobwebby wood and chicken wire structure that smelled strongly of dog food, poop, pee, and puppy breath. To me it was heaven. The dogs would come running to the wire, drowning out any other noise with their shrill beagle barks. I would put my fingers through the holes and let them lick and nip with their sharp puppy teeth. This is one of my most treasured memories of going up to "The Farm" as my dad called it.

So yes, he had the skills to help with a dog, just not the desire.

We had a lot of ups and downs with Phinny through the years. She was an incessant chewer. Telephone books, shoes, clothing, the linoleum, even my catcher's mitt were all fair game for her. She was also fiercely protective of the family. If anyone came to the door, she had to be held back by the collar, wanting to tear intruders to bits, snarling and snapping with the unbridled fury of a Tasmanian Devil. Many people came to the door back then, but Phinny reserved a particular deep hatred for Mr. Rosen.

It's anyone's guess what title would have been given to Mr. Rosen in the 60s. He was basically someone who extended credit to families that couldn't get a bank loan but would never go to a loan shark. He also arranged for furniture and appliances to be delivered at a discount from whatever the department store might charge. Mr. Rosen came to our house every Saturday morning like clockwork. Mom would leave money for him in an envelope by the door. I was generally the one who answered when he knocked, reluctantly stepping away from my Saturday morning cartoons. As I struggled with a lunging Phinny I would hand Mr. Rosen the envelope and he would count out whatever was in it, sometimes only five dollars, and jot it down on the "70 Jefferson" page in his small brown book. He was always very nice to me and tried every week to make friends with Phinny, only angering her further. He was a large, dark-skinned man with a deep booming voice. A terrifying monster to a little pup. On the Saturdays when the envelope was light, I was nervous that Mr. Rosen would tell me that it wasn't enough. I didn't know what I would do if he did, maybe offer my jar of change. It occurred to me a few years later that he most surely preferred small payments as it would draw Mom's debt out further and increase whatever interest he was charging. He must have been good at what he did. That little brown book of his was full and Joe Rosen came to our house for years.

Pawtucket didn't have a leash law at that time. Dogs roamed freely throughout our neighborhood wandering and doing dog stuff. Phinny was no exception. It seems absurd to me now, but we would just let her out the door. She developed a habit of sitting on the front stairs when she returned home and letting out short woofs until one of us let her back in. In retrospect it was terribly irresponsible of us to let an openly hostile dog roam freely. No one in the house gave any thought whatsoever to where she was going, where she was pooping, or who she was with. She was spayed and had her license and that made it alright in everyone's book. That is, until the police knocked on our door one night.

Somewhere along that day's travels, Phinny bit a young boy from the neighborhood. His family must have been familiar with her and where she lived. Maybe they saw her frequently sitting on the stairs doing her "Let me in" woofs. That night the officer knew just which door to knock on. As a young boy from a troubled area of Pawtucket my feelings about the police were that if a cop was talking to you, you must have done something wrong. As I watched my mom talking to him she looked weary, a kind of "what now" posture adopted from regularly dealing with work, bill collectors, aging parents, three girls, a boy, and my dad. She took the news gracefully as always. For reasons that I still don't understand, rather than requiring Phinny to be tied up or always on a leash, the officer said that if we wanted to keep her she had to wear a muzzle whenever she was out. He told Mom that if she hurt anyone else she would have to be "put down." I knew enough from Dad sometimes threatening this that I did not want it for my dog.

The next day, Mom came home with a small leather muzzle. She made the adjustments and put it on Phinny, flipping her ears forward as it went over her head. The dog seemed to take to it quickly and it soon became part of the ritual whenever she went out. It hung on a hook by the door. Phinny was very smart and would sit underneath it, telling us that she wanted to go out. She continued to roam the neighborhood at will, the only difference being that some people were afraid of her when they saw the muzzle. Over time the center strap would always slide over one eye, making her quite a peculiar sight, a kind of pirate dog walking the decks of Jefferson Avenue or sailing the Sea of Payne Park.

The years went by with Phinny. She never mellowed. She was my "growing up" dog and helped me through some difficult times. She followed me everywhere I went in the house and was a constant companion to me in my attic sanctuary, my refuge from the cramped space and sometimes chaotic events that occurred in the apartment below. As I got into my mid-teens I suppose that I was guilty of what any teenager would be at that point: paying more attention to the new experiences of a job, driving, high school, and the opposite sex than to my dog. Of course I still loved and cared for her, but she was such a steady presence in the house that I surely took her for granted.

One day I noticed that Phinny was limping a bit. I looked at her legs and feet and found an angry red growth between the pads on one of her back paws. I told my mom and showed it to her. At that point my dad was no longer able to work and was home all the time. He agreed to take her to Dr. Cournoyer the next day. I went off to school that morning and didn't think much more about it.

That night I got home after work and climbed the gray creaky stairs to our apartment. I let myself in and saw my mom's slightly hunched back, facing the sink washing dishes. I watched as she took a big deep breath. She turned to me, her voice breaking.

"Your doggie's gone."

"Gone wh—" Instantly sobbing, I went to her. She held me close, quietly crying herself. A torrent of emotions swept through me. I cried not only for the loss of my dog, my constant friend and companion, but for everything that had happened while we were together. The floodgates opened on years of loneliness and uncertainty, the illness that was chipping away at my dad, the constant insecurity that impaired my early teens, and seeing my sisters and my childhood friends moving forward without me. One thought kept coming back. Phinny was always there when I needed her. After all that she and I had been through together, I wasn't with her at the end. I didn't get to say goodbye.

My dad was never much for displays of emotion. As far as animals were concerned, they were just that — creatures meant to serve a purpose, do a job. But even Dad's voice broke a bit as he came into the kitchen.

"I'm sorry, Sam. There was nothing they could do."

I didn't go to him. Nor did he come to me. In an effort to let him know that I didn't blame him I quietly uttered, "I know, Dad."

I went up to my attic room. I didn't put on any music, didn't pick up a book or my drawing pad. I just kind of sat up there feeling empty. Mom had called one of my sisters and asked her to come by. She came up and quietly knocked. She tried to talk to me a bit, asked if I was going to be alright and gave me a hug. There was so much I wanted to say to her but I held it all in.

The next day dawned. Life went on, as it does. I went to school and work as I did every other day, trying not to think about Phinny.

My mom tried her best to ease my pain. She was a nurturing person to begin with and really just wanted to make me feel better. I guess I shouldn't have been surprised when I came home a week or so later to find a puppy waiting for me in the kitchen. Doing the only thing she could think to do, she went down to the Animal Rescue League after her shift and picked a puppy with the same coloring as Phinny, a black and brown female. I tried to feign joy but inside there were mixed emotions. Thoughts of her trying to replace my dog so quickly, feeling that I was somehow betraying Phinny by embracing a new puppy, a bit resentful that perhaps I might have wanted to pick my own dog, and guilt about being underwhelmed by her gesture all swirled through my head.

"I thought you would like to name her," my mom said. "She doesn't have one yet."

Looking up at the counter I saw an open box of Frosted Flakes still sitting there from breakfast. I christened her "Tony."

It was a sweet gesture, but Mom hadn't really thought it through. I was coming of age quickly and between school, work, and my friends I hardly had time to devote to training and bonding with a puppy. I tried my best but by nature teenage boys are almost entirely self-absorbed. Tony hung out at the house with my dad when I wasn't there. I made feeble efforts but she never really became my dog. I felt bad about it then but the solid reasoning of the universe became clear later on.

My life took an unexpected turn after my eighteenth birthday. Our mom endured many years of being ignored, slighted, taken for granted, and being left to care for her four children alone while Dad was at work, the bar, or in the company of friends. Unbeknownst to us, she had made a deal with herself years before. Simply put, once her youngest reached eighteen, she was leaving. In the spring after my birthday, she took me aside one day for a talk. She explained that she intended to honor the deal. I was free to stay with my dad in the only place I ever knew as home, or I could go with her. She'd already found an apartment with room for two. Despite my feelings of panic, there really wasn't much to think about. I had the choice of continuing to live with the person that had taken care of me throughout my life or stay with my dad, who needed frequent care and was just as frequently ungrateful. She'd already told him she was leaving but generously offered to continue to help him out with specifics like groceries, bill payments, and managing his medical care. We couldn't have a dog where we were going, and Dad agreed to keep Tony there with him on Jefferson Avenue.

The days leading up to us leaving were difficult. My dad repeatedly apologized, telling Mom he would die if she left and that he needed her. Too little, much too late. I don't recall packing anything, talking to my sisters about it, or having any strong feelings about going. I think I was just kind of numb that it was happening. Two memories that stand out have stayed with me all this time though. I went up to my attic room, my place of peace and comfort for so many years. It was a tough thing. A lot of me was there. The idea of letting that place go, my safe space, was difficult.

The other memory is of my dad lashing out at me the day we left. I honestly don't think he wanted to be mean, but at the time I was the nearest, easiest target. I didn't say anything back to him. I just stood there and took it, fighting tears once again. In the past I would have looked to my dog for love and comfort, but I didn't even know where Tony was during all of it.

From the point of that day, each of our roads split off in a different direction. Mom pushed through her guilt and strived to create a stable, calm life for herself, leaving me to handle my part on my own. Dad learned to care for himself and a dog in a second floor walkup apartment that formerly housed his family of six. With work and school on my plate I kept myself busy, pushing away the long-term implications and the weight of what we'd done by leaving.

And just as before, life went on.

A friend of my Dad's had a small house a few blocks away from Jefferson Avenue. There was a tiny makeshift apartment attached and he offered to rent it to my dad "dirt cheap." Seeking a more affordable place and almost certainly trying to escape the memories of the now-empty place where his family had once lived, he jumped at the opportunity. A few months after we left, George and Tony moved into an apartment right next door to my old school friends, Johnny and Jimmy LaVoie. Selfishly caught up in my own feelings about saying goodbye to my childhood home for good, I never once considered how it affected my father.

The apartment, and I call it that loosely, was a dark, dingy, depressing, brown box that for some reason had been sectioned off from the main house. It had a long narrow space reminiscent of a trailer with limited windows. From the first day I went by it seemed like he had moved into a place that the previous tenant had left just the day before, without cleaning it. I was appalled and to this day still feel ashamed that he lived there. It bothered my sisters and my mom too, but he himself never complained. I tried to make somewhat frequent visits to check on him and Tony and they always seemed fine. Once when I went by, my dad proudly showed me a photo that he had taken of Tony out in the yard.

"This is for you," he said, handing it over.

In the picture, Tony has the posture of a hunting dog, fiercely concentrating, nose pointed straight ahead, front leg raised. That my dad had the impetus to capture the moment still surprises me. I wonder how it came to be that he even had a camera loaded with film. The incident was very uncharacteristic of the person that I knew as my dad. Despite his feelings about animals, he had somehow connected with Tony. He was proud enough of her to take the picture and then have it enlarged for me. It was not like anything I'd seen from him before. I was oblivious to the idea that he might be trying to connect with me as well.

Near the Pawtucket/Central Falls line there was a high-rise, subsidized housing building. In keeping with the standards of the time, it wasn't horrible but it wasn't great either. My mom was adamant that dad couldn't keep living where he was and convinced him to put his name on the waiting list for Kennedy Manor on Broad Street. She was still taking care of him at this point, looking out for his wellbeing, monitoring his meds and doctor visits. I was generally unaware of all of it. I'm sure that she mentioned it to me, but it probably rolled off immediately. It certainly didn't occur to me that Tony couldn't live at Kennedy Manor with him.

His name came up quickly and he eventually agreed with my mom that it would be a better place to live. One day when I got home from work, she told me that he was moving and said we needed to talk about Tony. It suddenly dawned on me that my father would have to give her up and she would need a new home. I flashed back to that picture that he was so proud of and felt terrible. Before I could begin to process it, she took my hand.

"There's a boy who lives across the street from your dad. His name is Kenny and he is a special needs boy. Apparently he goes over to visit your dad and Tony every day after school. He really loves that dog. Your father wants to know if it's okay to ask his parents if Tony can go to live with them. You could still visit her, but she will be Kenny's dog."

I felt something breaking inside me. I knew that Tony was never truly my dog. Given the circumstances we never had the chance to bond that way. I felt sad, guilty, and deeply touched by the gesture my dad was making. I reigned in those feelings, ever aware of my mom's concern for me.

"That's good, Mom," I said with a hitch in my voice. "I'm really glad that she has a place to go where someone will love and care for her. Tell him it's okay."

As I went to my room, I pictured Dad talking to Kenny's parents with a chuckle. "She's a Heinz! 57 varieties!"

The move took place within the month. My dad didn't have much. The packing was done and cars loaded up in the space of a morning. We were getting ready to drive over to Kennedy Manor and leave that bleak, dismal apartment behind. I went out into the yard to see Tony.

"You're a good dog," I said with tears in my eyes, "You take care of that boy. He loves you and you're gonna have a good home. I'm sorry that I couldn't be better for you. Goodbye, girl."

I hugged her tightly and left. I knew I had to let go and decided not to visit Tony again. It hurt me too much to think about it and I was concerned that Kenny would fear that I was going to take her away. She was his dog now, and he was her person.

I know now that some dogs take a journey to get where they really belong. Along the way they may stop to fill a space where they are needed. Tony came to me through my mom's efforts to soothe my heartbreak. She became a companion to my dad during a painful and lonely time in his life, then found her true place as a best friend to a boy who would love her unconditionally.

When I was growing up, my father always put forth the idea that dogs are just work animals like cows, pigs, or chickens. Tony became much more to him than that. Did Tony change George, or just help to bring out what was already there? Along the way the little mongrel brought out a tenderness in him. I guess he was on a journey, too.

Years before, Dad might have stated that she would just have to go to the pound when he moved, end of story. With Tony he found enough empathy and compassion within himself to realize the good that could come from making a beautiful gesture to a small boy who needed her.

Rick Billings is an artist and writer from Pawtucket, Rhode Island. He has written and illustrated three children's picture books as well as a book of cartoons based on his experiences as a Firefighter/EMT. Contact Rick at bear59dog@yahoo.com

This story is dedicated to his dad.

Hope's Manifesto

— Laurie Heyden

Behind your defeated heart, an ember of hope resists the fading of light.
In this harsh and lonely world, survival has been your shield.
The weight of disappointments has deflected your gaze,
Turning your face from the warmth of the sun.

Self-criticisms hammer at the image you had of yourself,
As esteem leaks from your sad and weary eyes.
Your chin surrenders to the silent pull of gravity,
Blocking the light that would reveal your pain.

Mistaken conclusions of the past have trampled your spirit,
Imprinting a falsehood that runs deep to your core.
Discouragement has scribed a self-judgement of doubt,
Leaving you believing that you will never be enough.

Behind the mask that you don in defense as your fortress,
An inner you is burdened by fear as its cloak.
Your stubborn exterior defends a frightened soul,
Avoidant of failure, ridicule, and judgement.

An archenemy stands in your own two shoes.
Chipping at your ego like the marking of time,
Imprinting each undeserving self-assessment,
Leaving you believing that you are not enough.

Honesty declares this mask is not you.
Advocating at last with all of its power.
Tell fear to hold and self-condemnation to cease.
Swim no longer in an entanglement of self-deprecating lies.

The little voice of your conscience beckons from within,
Knowing the truth and aware of your own lies,
Salvaging the possibility that you are more than this.
If only you could show those boys who you really are.

Hope is the advocate and guardian of dreams;
And so, the little voice in your soul asks most sincerely,
"If the world would not laugh or put you down,
What hopes and dreams would you awaken?"

Dig deep and pull out the dreams tucked long from view.
Listen with an open heart to your soul's highest of plans.
Give dignity to the possibility that you so often, almost dis-
carded.
Dream big, then think even bigger.

A new purpose awaits when potential meets hope.
The possibility is as real as a butterfly's emergence.
When doubt takes over give a red light to fear.
Give yourself the green light to go for your passion.

You are an irreplaceable thread in this tapestry of humanity,
Uniquely equipped with your own constellation of gifts.
Your soul craves that you may see the true gifts within,
So, be true to the you, unique to yourself.

Hope is found in gratitude for all you are given,
So, practice a humble and gracious attitude.
Despite the simplicity or sophistication of your talents,
Speak of them in the affirmative and you will know grace.

In this deeply interconnected world, your presence was intentional.
Tune into the inner voice of truth and direction,
And have faith that within you await the answers and the way,
For authenticity is your new fortress and your strength.

Generously share your gifts with no regrets,
Despite that you may never know the impact of your goodness.
The universe holds beautiful possibilities for you. Hope will unlock them.
May your path be blessed with ease and joy, oh radiant soul!

Laurie Heyden, M.S., is a school psychologist, artist and jewelry designer who also writes inspirational literature.

"Hope's Manifesto" was inspired by her brother, Joey Ramos, who was a master at giving people the 'green light' to pursue their biggest dreams. Many of Joey's encouraging phrases, a.k.a. 'Mr. Ramos-isms,' are embedded in this prose poem.

Assisting the Living

— Tom Barr

E dward Yellen unbuckled his seatbelt and looked through the windshield at a sign that said Woodbrook Assisted Living Center. His son, Mark, got out of the driver's seat and walked around the car to open Edward's door. Edward rotated awkwardly, and his feet alighted on the concrete surface beneath a porte-cochère. As he stood, he farted, in a curious harmony with the idling engine.

Edward's wife, Ruth, emerged from the rear seat and said with a sigh, "Oh, Edward."

"You should be used to it by now, Mom," Mark said. "Are you okay to walk in with him while I park the car?"

"Of course." She tugged on Edward's short sleeve, and he tottered forward with her. A hot midsummer breeze swept through the shaded entryway. "Edward, do you remember why we're here?"

"Huh," Edward said.

"Do you remember why we are here?" she said with more space between the words, but no louder.

"No."

"We talked all morning about it, honey. We came to visit my cousin Florence."

"Huh?" he said again, cupping his hand behind one ear and squinting simultaneously.

75

Ruth walked erect, took Edward's slow pace, and did not immediately answer. It was as though she had shouted her prior answer across a field and was waiting for an acknowledgement delayed by the speed of sound. "It's been over a year since we've seen Florence. I'd like to know what she thinks of this place."

Ruth and Edward approached the automatic sliding doors and then walked through the wave of air-conditioned air that sloshed out when they opened. Mark joined them, and the doors slid shut behind.

"Where's here?" Edward asked.

"Wood-brook As-sist-ed Liv-ing," Mark said. "We're in Bristol."

"Bristol?" Edward said, squinting and cupping his hand again.

"Yes, Dad. That's right. Bristol, Rhode Island."

"Don't you live here?" Edward asked.

"No. I live in Bristol, Virginia," Mark replied, his voice raised to his father. A bemused expression crossed his face. "I'm just visiting you and Mom for a couple of weeks. She asked me to be here to help with some decisions."

"Uh huh."

Mark turned to his mother. "He was always interested in places and driving between them, and he almost had that bit of data right."

"It comes out of nowhere, but less often these days," Ruth said, speaking in a comparably low voice. "Listen, I'm glad you could come with us today. By the way, did you bring that bag for Florence?"

"Yep. Peanut butter cookies. They smell great."

"Be glad," Ruth said, "that you've still got your sense of smell. Your dad lost his. Evidently, that goes along with…his condition."

Ruth and Edward walked side by side, he slowly, with a sustained scowl, and she upright with her wavy gray hair clipped in the back. Mark followed. She smiled at a family coming down the hall, but

Edward kept his eyes to the floor, as if expecting to step over something.

"Where's my cane?" Edward asked.

"You'll be all right without it for this short distance," Ruth replied.

"Oh."

"There's the directory," Mark said.

"No need for that," Ruth said. "I know Florence's number—138."

At the desk, the receptionist asked their names and whom they were visiting. She printed three tags, which Ruth and Mark stuck to their shirts. Edward fumbled trying to peel off the backing, and Mark watched for several seconds before doing it for him and sticking the tag on his father's plaid shirt.

Though his mother had dismissed the directory, Mark stepped closer to it. In a wood-framed glass case labeled "Residents," four 8-1/2 by 11 sheets were stapled to a corkboard, each with July 24, 2011 in the footer.

"Looks as if this was updated only a few days ago," Mark said.

"They probably have to do that weekly," Ruth said with a brief grimace. "And actually, as I say that, I should have a look." She drew up beside her son and scanned the lists. "Hmm. Here's a name I've not seen in a while."

"Who's that?" Mark asked.

"Gladys Anderson," Ruth said. "She was your dad's first-grade teacher."

"Wait. What? Hold on," Mark said, his eyebrows raised. "Did you say what I thought I heard you say?"

"I believe I said what I meant," Ruth said.

"Dad's first-grade teacher," Mark repeated. "How is that possible? He's eighty-four years old. Wouldn't that mean…." Mark's expression of bewilderment persisted.

"Gladys is almost a hundred," Ruth said. "Last I knew, she was living by herself in the house where her parents used to live. She's been self-sufficient all along, so she must've only recently moved here."

"Okay. So maybe that works out with the ages. She's sixteen years older than he is, so when he was six, she was twenty-two," Mark said. "Is my arithmetic correct?"

"Yes, that's right. It is possible. My goodness, by the time you're a hundred, you may be ready for somebody else to do the cooking and cleaning. That must be why she moved." Ruth examined her son's expression. "You still don't believe me? Tell you what. We'll go see her, after we spend a few minutes with Florence."

"How do you know all this? About Gladys. And about Dad?" Mark asked.

"Well, we are from around here, and of a time when people kept up with each other. We've lived other places, but—unlike you—we eventually settled back here. It's hard *not* to know about people when you're in the same community for decades."

Ruth and Mark talked loudly enough for Edward to hear, but he had stood still beside them, watching activity in the lobby. People bent with age—almost all women—sat on sofas or scuffled along behind walkers. His gaze seemed fixed on a Black woman with close-cropped, gray hair and dark-rimmed glasses who was seated at a card table playing rummy with a pale, bony woman whose hair looked like a loose cotton ball.

Ruth tugged on Edward's sleeve to direct him, and the three walked along a corridor with a floor glossy from recent mopping.

"So, clearly, Dad's gotten worse," Mark said.

"I'm sure the change is obvious to you, since it's been—what—a year since you were last here," Ruth said. "I'm getting worried about what's to come. How will I be able to deal with him?"

"I don't think he has any idea of the real reason we came to Woodbrook today."

Edward's crepe soles squeaked on the polished concrete floors, echoing down the hall.

"I'm glad you're here now. When you're in only for a few days at a time, though, it's hard for me to remember all the things I want to talk about. I really hope you'll call or visit more often," Ruth said, with less cheer in her voice.

"I have to live where there's work. I can't just uproot and move," Mark began.

"We're not having that conversation now," Ruth replied. "Sorry I brought it up."

Mark and Ruth were three doors from 138, and they paced Edward's slow, scuffling gait.

"I need to sit down," Edward said.

"See that door up there with the picture of fireworks on it," Mark said, stepping in front of his father and pointing.

"No."

"Just take my word, that's Florence's. We are almost there, and you can sit in her apartment."

Ruth and Mark stopped in front of the door, and she grasped the back of Edward's shirt to signal he shouldn't go any farther. She turned to her son and said, "One other thing I've learned from my readings about Alzheimer's."

"What?"

"It's heritable."

"Thanks for that cheerful insight, Mom."

In addition to a letter-size poster showing fireworks exploding over a cityscape, Florence's door was festooned with a few Independence Day cards. Ruth opened one, which was signed by a handful of women from Florence's church. When they entered the apartment, Ruth locked eyes with Florence, and the two women exchanged hugs.

"To what do I owe the honor?" Florence asked, her wrinkled but corpulent face reshaping to a broad smile.

Ruth held her cousin's hands and looked her in the eye. "Truth be told, you're one of my last living relatives, and…"

"Makes you one of my last ones as well," Florence replied, still smiling. She surveyed Ruth through her thick glasses and laughed. "You've not changed. You don't look like you weigh a pound more than you did forty years ago."

"Well, here's no news to you. You always had me beat in that category," Ruth said.

"Ah, same old Ruth. Calls 'em as you sees 'em. And of course, Mark you must understand, your mother and I have always teased each other. Her ears, well, you know, they could be used for flying."

Mark proffered the cookies to Florence, with a little hesitation.

"Thank you!" Florence said. "Food in the café here is okay, but desserts leave a lot to be desired. These'll be a perfect antidote. Now, sit, sit, and sit," she said to Ruth, Edward, and Mark. They complied, and Edward laid his hat on the sofa arm.

The conversation, mostly between the two women, began with their health. All things considered, things were not too bad either for Ruth, in her late seventies, or for Florence, close to ninety. They spoke of other relatives and common friends—some sick, some dead, and some who by their reckoning were doing all right.

Trying to engage with Edward, Florence said, "Edward, how are you?"

He looked at her with bewilderment, cupped his hand to his ear, and said, "What?"

"How. Have. You. Been?" Florence said.

"Fine," he replied.

"Dad's gotten hard of hearing and remembering," Mark said, as if to explain his situation to Florence.

"No need to interpret for me," Florence said. "Plenty of it among the residents here." Ruth commented on Florence's long, thick sweater, not a garment she'd expect to see her wearing in July. Florence opined that the place had lately been over-air-conditioned. They had installed a new system, and the management had not yet figured out how to run it properly.

"Actually," Ruth said, "Edward likes to have it cold indoors in the summer." Ruth asked about the heating, and Florence had plenty to say about being cold in the winter as well, and not being able to adjust her own room's temperature independently.

"In the winter, it's a different story," Ruth said. "Edward prefers it toasty."

"You'd never get 'toasty' here," Florence said with a laugh. "If I read you right, you're thinking of moving Edward to some place like this?"

"I don't know what I'm thinking," Ruth said. "I do worry about the future. He won't get better. And if it's just me with him to take care of in that house. It would be expensive for both of us to live here…" She trailed off. "Edward has no idea. Thank goodness he's so hard of hearing."

Edward took a couple of tries at pushing himself up out of his chair and finally stood, hat in hand. "Are we ready to go?" he asked.

Ruth said, "Edward, please, can you sit just a few more minutes?"

"I'm ready," he said, still standing. He put on his cap and adjusted it on his bald head.

"Dad! Don't you want to stay a bit longer? We just got here."

"I want to GO!" Edward shouted in a wheezy voice.

Ruth cast a pleading look at her cousin and said, "Looks as if we need to come back another time. Hope they get the AC fixed. I want to hear more about what it's like to live here. Maybe I'll give you a call."

Once they were in the hall, Ruth said quietly to Mark, "It was cold in there. So aggravating. I think this expedition is just about over. Let's go to the car."

Ruth tugged on Edward's sleeve and spoke more loudly to him, "All right. Let's go. This way."

As they moved down the hall toward the elevators, Edward looked at his son, eyebrows arched and asked, "How old am I?"

Mark gave a quizzical look at his mother as if to say, 'Do you want me to handle this one?'

She nodded 'yes,' and Mark turned to his dad. "You're now eighty-four."

"Eighty-four?" Edward echoed, continuing to arch his eyebrows and looking down at the floor. "That's old."

"Not as old as some," Mark said. "We were going to see Gladys Anderson. She's about sixteen years older than you are."

"We're going to see Miss Anderson now," Edward said.

Mark and Ruth exchanged astonished expressions. "After that outburst, I thought we should go home."

"We'll go," Edward said, his voice rising as it had moments earlier, "to see Miss Anderson!"

Ruth and Mark were speechless.

"She was my first-grade teacher. I want to see her."

The Yellens rode the elevator to the second floor, and when they exited, their pace was a bit less tentative than it had been on the floor below. Edward followed his wife and son without prompting. Mark knocked at 281.

An aged, strong soprano voice said, "Come in." Gladys Anderson was seated with a straight back in a captain's chair. Her hair was white, pulled back in a bun, and she wore glasses with dark blue frames. Her makeup was light, and her alert, cheerful countenance made it seem she was decades younger than her near-century age. She laid a book aside on the table next to her.

"Hello, Edward. And Ruth!" she said without hesitation. "What a nice surprise. How long has it been? And who is this with you?"

"I'm their son, Mark. Pleased to meet you, Miss Anderson."

"Mark, just call me Gladys," she said. "Or at least Ms. That 'miss' stuff is from when your dad was a kid." Gladys gestured toward a love seat and a large stuffed chair.

"Mark's in town for a few days from his home in Virginia," Ruth said. "We came to Woodbrook today…to see my cousin Florence. But when we saw your name on the residents list, we wanted to add you in."

"Mom—and, well, Dad too—said you were his first-grade teacher."

"Yes, indeed. Edward was in one of my first classes. You remember your first students the best. They're the ones that form you the most as a teacher."

"Last I'd heard," Ruth interrupted, "you were living at your home place, so it was a little surprising to see your name on the resident list. Are you all right?" Ruth asked.

"My niece was worried about me living alone, and she finally talked me into moving here. It's not the same, but I'm making it."

Addressing Mark, Gladys said, "Most of my adult life I've lived and worked in these parts. I did spend a couple of years at Teachers College at Columbia for a masters." Turning to Ruth, she continued, "Ah, yes, I see Florence regularly in the dining room. Sometimes she'll sit at the same table with me. Complains about the food, and lately about the air conditioning." Gladys then smiled and spoke to Edward. "And what about you, young man? How have you been?"

Ruth and Mark both were about to answer for him, but Edward looked at Gladys with interest and said, "Fine." Mark and Ruth inhaled as if readying to take up for him, but he continued, "Good to hear you're all right, Miss Anderson."

"Well, now, Edward, you're grown up and entitled to call me by my first name."

"All right. Gladys."

Gladys and Edward exchanged a few more words, and the other two traded wide-eyed glances. Edward's face lightened and he spoke in short, complete sentences in a halting back-and-forth with Gladys.

At a momentary lull in their conversation, Ruth started to explain Edward's situation, and got as far as the word "dementia."

He gave her a look of annoyance and said, "I...." and Ruth stopped.

"Edward?" Gladys said.

"Yes, um, Gladys," Edward replied.

Mark started to say something.

Edward interrupted his son. "I'm fine, as I said. Well, other than this Alzheimer's business. Not sure what's going to happen there."

Gladys said, "There's plenty of that at Woodbrook. I've been here long enough to see it just starting, advanced, and in between. Ruth was just starting to tell me about it."

"It's happening, but I don't like to talk about it," Edward said. He paused and looked intently at Gladys's right ear. "Are those clip-on earrings?"

Silence reigned for several seconds at this seeming non sequitur.

"Why, yes, they are," Gladys said.

"You used to wear clip-ons," Edward said.

Again, there was a long pause.

"I did," Gladys said. "Why do you mention it?"

"I remember," Edward started. "I remember when I was in your class and they'd sometimes fall off. You would have us hunt for them under the desks."

"You're right, Edward!" Gladys said. "That must have made an impression to last, what, almost eighty years or so."

"Yes," he said.

Once again, Edward seemed to retreat from the conversation. He was quiet while the other three filled the air with talk of local connections and Ruth's increasing burden as a caregiver. Edward squinted a bit, staring at the table beside Gladys.

At another quiet moment, Gladys noticed Edward staring beside her chair and asked, "What do you see?"

"What's the book you're reading?" Edward asked, sounding genuinely curious.

Ruth and Mark exchanged a sidelong glance.

"Glad you asked me, Edward. It's a biography of Alexander Hamilton. Came out, oh, several years ago, and I'd been meaning to get to it, but somehow other things drew my attention."

Edward sat quietly for a few seconds, as if the words were coming from a great distance, and then he said, "I read it when it was first published."

Gladys was unfazed, but Mark and Ruth seemed astonished at each turn.

"How long ago was that, Ruth?" Edward continued.

"Maybe 2004," Ruth said.

"Glad to know your scholarly interests have continued," Gladys said. "Even when you were little, you were keen to learn to read."

Edward continued. "I remember you sitting at your desk at the front of our classroom, and sometimes you wore a flowered dress. It had dahlias on it." Edward trailed off, and just as Gladys was about to reply he asked, "When was I in your class?" he asked.

Mark and Ruth continued to sit quietly on the shore of this little island of lucidity where Edward had run aground.

"Why, Edward, that would have been—let me think—about nineteen thirty-three. Yes, I think that's it, because I finished college in '32, and started teaching that fall. You were in my second class of first graders." Gladys continued, "I had just the previous fall voted for the first time in a presidential election. It wasn't more than a dozen years after the nineteenth amendment. Mother wanted to be sure I didn't miss my first opportunity."

Edward asked, "Who did you vote for?"

"Why, FDR, of course. Mother and Dad were yellow dogs. I still am, though looking around this place, I know I'm a dying breed." Gladys gestured by spreading her thin arms in both directions to indicate the Woodbrook facility.

"That's what I thought," Edward said. "You know, I used to be involved in politics."

"Yes, I do, actually. You helped with Cleve Burns's campaign for the state legislature. Got the teachers in the state to pay attention. Helped keep him focused on teacher pay. He won three terms thanks to you and the little group you got together," Gladys said.

"That was an awful lot of work," Edward said. "But we made progress. Now, he's gone, and a lot of the others who were involved are gone, too. I'm one of the last."

Ruth started to intervene in the conversation, perhaps to protest Edward's fatalistic statement.

Gladys spared her. "Now, Edward. You're just a youngster. That's how you'll always be in my mind. When you were in the first grade, you were serious and obedient. I never had to call you down. You had such an interest in handwriting, and yours was the best in the class. I can't say the same thing about your spelling, however."

"He's still not a good speller," Mark interjected.

"So, you see," Gladys said, "some things haven't changed since 1933."

"Any other things you recall about Dad?" Mark asked.

"Oh yes. Probably shouldn't tell you this. But I am old, and I won't get too many more chances to lay things out as I saw them. Your dad," she spoke to Mark, "was shy, even nervous, and didn't want to play with the other kids. He would wander along the edge of the playground at recess and avoided getting into the pickup ballgames. It bothered me, and I would go out and walk beside him sometimes. He would tolerate that. He even seemed to prefer the company of someone older."

"I don't remember things that way," Edward said.

"Oh, you were very much like that," Gladys said. "You may have been the one who always wanted to please the teacher, at least in the classroom, but you were a problem child in some ways. I tried to talk with you. Even went to your mother once. She just said, 'That's Edward.' She already seemed resigned to the way you were." Gladys looked toward Mark and Ruth with a questioning expression, as if she wanted to tell them something but wasn't sure she should in Edward's presence.

"You remind me of Mother," Edward said. "She's been gone a long time, too."

"When did your mother pass away?" Gladys asked.

"It was in the eighties. She was old," Edward said.

"And when were you born?" Gladys asked.

"Nineteen twenty-seven," Edward answered, without hesitation. "I was born in New Mexico, and then Mother and Dad moved to southwest Virginia when I was three. When I started high school, they moved us to Rhode Island, and I've been here ever since."

"Well, here's a little fact for you. I was born before New Mexico was a state!" Gladys said, grinning widely. "What do you think about that?"

"You *must* be old," Edward replied.

The whole group chuckled.

"Yes, child. Not too many get to the century mark. And even fewer get much past that," Gladys said, with a twinge of resignation in her voice.

Edward and Gladys talked for half an hour, trading questions and answers, sometimes disputing one another's claims, and other times nodding with smiles and happiness about times of childhood or of young adulthood. Gladys traced her experiences of the thirties and forties—listening to local radio shows and national broadcasts like *Amos 'n' Andy*, seeing the Depression play out in a town of ten thousand, teaching, going off to New York for graduate school, returning to Rhode Island to teach history, the Second World War.

Edward related his own story through that period and described his disappointment at not being old enough to go to war before it was over. He did, it turned out, get his turn by serving in the Korean conflict. Edward traced his own career as an English teacher in the public schools starting in the fifties. As the minutes wore on, Edward spoke of more recent events, and while Gladys affirmed he had been a regular at the annual retired teachers' luncheons, she corrected his calling the wrong names for former colleagues. He couldn't recall his grandchildren's names. After a few more minutes, the sunshine that had risen in his face and voice faded. The gray clouds of forgetfulness and confusion rolled back in. After a few more minutes, the talk ground to a halt. Each of the four staring, not at each other, but at some point in the air in front of them.

Gladys rose and motioned Mark and Ruth to come with her to her tiny bedroom. Edward sat motionless, looking ahead with a disinterest deeper than when they were downstairs in Florence's apartment.

"There's something I think you should know," Gladys said to Ruth and Mark. "When I say that Edward was shy and retiring as a youngster, I'm understating. He was what they'd now call clinically depressed. In all my years before and after him, I never saw it quite that bad in any other children I taught."

"That doesn't surprise me," Ruth said. "He's had bouts of it. Even had prescriptions for years at a time."

"What?" Mark said. "Here's more, Mom, you haven't told me."

"Surely you noticed," Ruth replied. "Or, well, maybe not. Perhaps he stayed that way steadily enough that you children thought of it as the norm. This is all of a piece, though."

"How's that?" Mark asked.

"I've read enough about dementia to know that it often goes along with depression earlier in life. I've seen plenty of it in Edward's midlife. And Gladys just confirmed how longstanding it's been."

"Oh, you don't know the worst of it," Gladys said, her centenarian eyes now betraying their age. She sat down abruptly on the side of her bed, her featherweight body lightly indenting the white chenille bedspread. The other two sat beside her.

"Are you all right?" Ruth asked.

Gladys nodded, but she looked steadily before her without making eye contact with Ruth or Mark.

Mark said, "What happened?"

"Nothing just now, other than my realizing I should tell you this."

"Tell us what?" Mark asked.

"One day," Gladys said, "at the end of recess, all of my other children were headed back into the building, but I saw your father going the other direction, and well beyond the playground. He was headed for the train tracks. I yelled to him, and he didn't stop or respond. He had been particularly unhappy that day, and cried. I knew something was terribly wrong, and I ran after him. As it happened, there was a train approaching, and he seemed all the more determined. Never have I run so hard in my life. I managed to grab his arm, when he was within just a few feet of the tracks. A few more seconds, and he would have been on them, in front of the train."

Ruth and Mark were dry-eyed, and ashen. The cuckoo clock on the wall ticked. Gladys's mouth was slightly open, and the papery skin on the back of her fingers stretched as she clasped Ruth's hand. White noise from the air conditioning vent was the only other sound until they heard Edward get up from his chair and begin scuffling around the adjacent room.

"So," Mark said, "I have you to thank for my..."

90

"Your existence?" Gladys finished his sentence.

"I suppose." Mark's face was pale. "I need to go tend to Dad." He left the room.

"I know, dear, why you really came today."

Ruth grimaced and started to cry. "It's obvious?"

"He would do fine here. And it would make your life so much better," Gladys said. "I could tell you hadn't seen anything like what happened here today. Those lucid moments just appear, but they get rarer and rarer. What comes next is much worse. You want all the help you can get with that."

"I don't know what to say."

"No need," Gladys said. "We can't avoid our burdens, but we can share them."

They rose and joined Mark and Edward in the other room.

"We'll need to get home so I can fix supper," Ruth said. Turning to Gladys, she said, "It was good to see you. Thank you for drawing Edward out."

"Nothing I did on purpose. My pleasure to have you stop in," Gladys said, her voice sounding weaker, drained.

"Edward, I hope you stay well," Gladys said.

Edward said nothing.

"Dad, your hat," Mark said, pointing to the love seat arm. Without a response from Edward, Mark picked it up and handed it to his father.

Ruth tugged on Edward's sleeve as before. He didn't lift his feet much as he took a few steps forward. The three—father, mother, son—retraced their steps through the Woodbrook Center. At the exterior door, Mark ran to fetch the car. He pulled it to the same spot in front of the automatic door and helped his father in.

Mark drove his parents toward their house, with the windows down and the hot, humid summer air flowing into the passenger compartment. During the trip, Edward watched out the window, and Ruth commented on how good the warm air felt in comparison with the filtered and chilled air inside the nursing home.

"Mark," Ruth said, "do you think it's time your dad and I sell the house and move to some place like Woodbrook?"

"That's a big question," Mark said, momentarily gripping the steering wheel tighter. "You've been in this place for, what, fifty-five years? It'd be an undertaking to sort through stuff and get moved."

"Yes. But you see how your dad is, and how things are changing. I'm just not sure how I'll be able to deal with it on my own." Her voice quavered, tinged with fear.

Mark turned at St. Jude's Church onto his parents' street and drove slowly along the tree-lined way. Dogwoods dotted the green median. They approached the wide, one-story ranch-style Yellen home, and then pulled into the driveway. Mark walked around to the right-hand side of the car to open the doors for his mother and father. They both emerged into the mid-afternoon summer sun, and the metal in the car's engine emitted a light, periodic 'tink' as it cooled.

Edward surveyed the exterior facade of brick and clapboard nestled behind pruned boxwoods and yews. His eyes widened, and without turning toward Ruth or Mark, who stood on either side of him, he said, "I've never seen this place before. But it is beautiful. Why are we here?"

Tom Barr is the author of a memoir (in search of a publisher), and longer-term of academic textbooks. Currently, he is focusing on short stories, many of which are themed on loss--of love, mobility, memory, freedom, and life. The beneficiary of a rural upbringing, he has had a career as a mathematician and enjoys writing characters who experience the world in both humanistic and scientific terms. He and his wife Kathryn live in Providence, Rhode Island.

The High Fructose Corn Syrup Debacle

— Mike Squatrito

"It worked!" I exclaimed, shocked at the outcome of my latest experiment. Now to crunch the numbers.

"What are you doing, Chase?" asked my wife. She always appears at the wrong time.

"You're never going to believe what I just accomplished!" I beamed. "Want to go for a ride?"

Jaime tilted her head and pointed at the spherical machine. "In that thing?"

I gazed at my masterpiece and smiled. "Yes, in that."

"What is it?" she asked, placing her hands on her hips, unamused.

"Um, a time machine," I said, matter-of-factly. "I just came back from my maiden voyage. Everything checked out fine!"

"What are you talking about?" she asked, scrunching her brow. "You've been in and out of the garage all morning."

"It's a time machine," I reiterated. "You didn't know I was gone because I set the return time to be one second after I left."

Jaime rolled her eyes. I knew I had precious little time to convince her to come with me. Time to pull out the big guns. "You know I'm an astrophysicist, right? I really invented something remarkable."

Shaking her head, she relented and said, "Show me what you made."

I could barely contain the excitement in my thirty-year-old frame. Opening the compartment door, I extended my hand and said, "Climb in. There's room for two but it's a little tight."

Jaime hesitated at first, then peeked her head inside the contraption. To my surprise, she scrunched down and ventured inside, maneuvering into the passenger's seat. I followed, closed the cabin door behind me, and sat in the captain's chair.

Panning, she analyzed the dashboard panel and instrumentation, but the three-hundred-and-sixty-degree view impressed her the most. "Not bad, Chase," she said, pursing her lips and raising her eyebrows.

I buckled up and she did the same. Next, I started flipping switches and checked my instruments. Jamie witnessed my actions. Waving her hands, she said, "Hold on! Before we go anywhere, you need to tell me what all of this is about."

"Good point," I said. Pointing to the dashboard, I continued. "These instruments are kind of like the ones in a car." Motioning to each in order, I said, "This one's the speedometer, propulsion system checks, altimeter, and time and spatial coordinates."

"All right," she said, skepticism in her voice. "Is there enough fuel in the tank?"

Fuel! I love her! "This runs on a propulsion system, not an engine like our cars," I said. "The time machine uses the magnetism of the Earth, combined with laser-directed isotopic reactions and a rotating hull to open a portal in space–time. And everything's activated by using an AI voice recognition system."

"So, we're going back in time?"

"Or forward," I said. "Technically, we're entering the fourth dimension, which is time. From there, we can slide back into the past or forward into the future."

Jaime's face went blank. "Right ..." she said, her voice trailing off. "Um, where or when are we going?"

A wide smile stretched across my face. "I just came back from the Jurassic Period! We can go back to see some dinosaurs. It's amazing!"

"Sounds good," she said, folding her arms across her chest.

"Or we can go to the Cretaceous Period and see a Tyrannosaurus battle a Triceratops!"

"When did that asteroid hit the Earth? You know, the one that wiped them all out?" Jaime raised an eyebrow.

"Yeah, I'm not sure of the exact date and time. Maybe we should skip that trip for now." Note to self: stay away from apocalyptic events.

"Alicia, set time coordinates to previous excursion," I said, enacting the AI system.

"Welcome back, Chase," said the sultry female voice with an Australian accent. "Setting coordinates to North America, 100 million years ago."

Jaime shot me a look of disapproval. "Really? Alicia? Wasn't that the name of an old girlfriend of yours?"

I flashed a sheepish smile. "That didn't last, honey. I married you." Note to self: do not name voice interfaces after ex-girlfriends.

"Alicia, activate system and begin time sequence," I commanded from my captain's chair.

Both of us looked out the all-encompassing windshield, finding our backyard, house, and all our belongings sitting in their respective places, undisturbed. A soft hum emanated from the vehicle.

"Alicia, system update," I said.

"All systems are go," responded the AI voice. "Commencing countdown. Sixty seconds to activation."

I turned to my wife. "After everything fires up, we'll be able to glide across the sky like a hockey puck on ice."

"Will anything see us?"

"No! This machine is in perpetual stealth mode. We don't want anyone or anything to see or hear us, and we definitely don't want to interact with them," I said in the most serious voice I possessed. "I don't want to be responsible for some exotic Butterfly Effect catastrophe."

"Makes sense," said Jaime.

"Thirty seconds," came Alicia's smooth voice.

Jaime peered over to my chair. Scrunching her brow, she said, "Is that a Coke in a cup holder?"

I looked down at the open twenty-ounce container. "Think of this as the ultimate road trip. I always enjoy something to drink whenever we visit a zoo or museum or take a long drive."

"You're going to need to pee," deadpanned Jaime. Panning the cockpit, she added, "I don't see any restroom in this thing."

I gave her a blank stare. "I'll hold it." Note to self: add human waste elimination subsystem to next round of vehicle modifications.

"Three, two, one," said Alicia. The outside spun at a tremendous rate, but we felt nothing inside our anti-gravity compartment. Next, a rip in space-time appeared in front of our craft.

"Preparing to enter portal," said Alicia.

The time capsule moved into the empty hole, then zipped further through the void. Resembling a wormhole with darkness and streaking stars, my invention hurtled into the fourth dimension and back in time. Seconds later, Alicia's voice filled the compartment again.

"South Dakota, North America, 100 million years ago."

"We're not going to run into anything, are we?" asked Jaime.

"No," I said, gripping the controls in front of me. "I can maneuver the craft using this."

"I mean, we're high enough up in the sky to not hit a building, plane, or in this case a flyer dinosaur, right?"

My eyebrows grew high on my forehead. "Of course we are," I lied. Note to self: add altitude to initial insertion parameters. Preferably 10,000 feet.

The panoramic windshield changed from streaming darkness to bright light. The sun shone from above and the blue sky filled our view screen as I continued to use the controls to steer the ship.

Gazing at my instruments, I relayed what they displayed. "Our speed is 100 miles per hour and we're about 5,000 feet above sea level. The time is 12:34 PM, our time. I mean, there are no clocks here!"

Jaime surveyed the landscape from her seat. Lush flora rose from the ground, the plants' leaves immense. "Look at all the vegetation," she said, unbridled awe in her voice. "Where are the dinosaurs?"

"I'll descend and slow us down," I said, lowering the craft to about a hundred feet above the surface and to a reasonable speed of ten miles an hour.

"Outside temperature is eighty-seven degrees Fahrenheit with relative humidity at 77 percent," said Alicia.

"Florida weather!" I exclaimed. Panning the outside view, I did my best to find some of the elusive animals. Seconds later, I found what we came to see.

Pointing to my left, I shouted, "Over there! A herd of brachiosaurus!"

Jamie leaned forward, craning her neck to get a better view. Her eyes grew round. "Oh, my God," she said, her mouth remaining open in shock. "Those are really dinosaurs!"

I brought the craft closer to the herd, getting about ten feet above the beasts. The adults moved the herd forward, while younger brachiosaurs used their long necks to pluck huge leaves from the trees.

"This is simply amazing," I said, still riveted to the scene before me, even though I had witnessed the same thing on my previous trip.

Jaime shook her head. "Babe, I underestimated you."

I sat up a bit higher in my seat. "Let's find some more dinosaurs."

Using the controls, I hit the thrusters and swung the craft to the right of the herd, heading toward an area with less vegetation. Our next target revealed itself right in front of us.

"Stegosauruses!" I beamed.

Jaime's eyes stayed wide. "I can't believe this," she said, shaking her head. The huge beasts with their massive back plates and spiked tails were unmistakable.

"Alicia, is the video camera recording?" I asked.

"Video is operational and set on by default," answered the AI voice.

"We'll have all the proof we need for the world to believe us," I said.

"I know this is surreal, but how long are we staying here?" asked Jaime. "We're not going to arrive home thousands of years in the future, are we?"

"Of course not," I said. "I designed this machine to return a second after we departed."

Jaime smiled, then looked out the windshield again, taking in the panoramic view one last time. "This is enough for me for now, but I'd love to go on another trip again."

"Oh, we will, Jaime, we will," I said. "I'll start our return journey." Before initiating the return sequence, I took another long look at the Earth from 100 million years ago.

A sense of calmness overtook my body, and my entire consciousness filled with bliss. "Can you believe all of this?" I said, spreading my arms wide for emphasis. To my chagrin, I smacked the open Coke bottle with my hand, spilling its syrupy contents onto the dashboard.

Jaime instinctively lifted up in her seat, trying to avoid getting the carbonated brown liquid on her shorts. The soda rolled into a couple of crevices in the dashboard, causing pops and snaps to fill the cockpit.

"What was that?" exclaimed Jaime, her heart racing.

"Uh-oh," I said, grabbing the bottle and placing it upright in its holder.

Jaime panned the interior. Staring at me with an incredulous look, she asked, "Don't you have any napkins or towels?"

I didn't. "No," I said. "I never thought I'd need Wet-Naps or anything like that!"

Jaime stripped off her T-shirt and dabbed the dashboard, the cloth soaking up the liquid.

Staring at my wife's now semi-bare upper body, I commented, "Is that one of your sexy bras?"

Jaime shot me a look of exasperation. "Really, Chase? Really?"

I shook my head, snapping myself out of my stupor. "Sorry! My bad!" Non-technical note to self: Jaime was a lot more fun as a girlfriend, not so much as a wife.

"Alicia, run diagnostics," I said, trying to stave off a panic attack.

"Stealth system compromised," said Alicia.

Jaime glared at me. "What did she mean by that?"

I stared out the windshield. The time machine hovered ten feet above three stegosauruses. The dinosaurs lifted their stubby necks and gazed upwards.

"Oh no," I said. "They're looking at us!"

"They can *see* us?" said Jaime. "Are our shields down?"

"Yeah, this isn't good," I said, ignoring her cute Star Trek reference and pulling up on the console, taking the craft upwards. I then turned the vehicle west and toward the herd of brachiosaurus. A few of the larger animals focused on our ship, trumpeting in protest.

As I tried to maneuver away, the craft decided to stay on course. "Manual operations compromised," said Alicia.

"Shit!" I exclaimed.

"You and your goddamn Coke!" shrieked Jaime. "Can this thing fly on its own?"

"Alicia, initiate autopilot," I commanded.

"Autopilot engaged."

The time machine hurtled closer to a larger member of the herd, approaching five feet from its huge head. Jaime and I held our breath as the beast's face filled the viewport. Alicia pulled the craft upward and out of the animal's path in the nick of time.

"Chase, get us out of here!" yelled Jaime.

"Alicia, return home," I ordered. "Time coordinates now!"

The AI brain initiated the return sequence. As it did, the world outside the spacecraft started to swirl. A void in space-time opened again. Just as the vehicle entered the portal, we both heard an electrical snap under the dashboard.

Jamie crossed her arms over her almost bare breasts. "Fucking soda!" she said, shooting me another death stare.

Outside, the view brightened. "South Africa, 1:37 PM, April 18, 1967," said Alicia.

"What?" I exclaimed. "No, no, no! Alicia, return home immediately!"

The AI machine attempted another jump in time; however, the little craft began to zigzag up and down, then left and right for a few seconds.

"Initiating return sequence," said Alicia.

Again, the fabric of space-time opened, the ship went into the void and popped out a fraction of a second later. "Saunderstown, USA, 4:51 PM, March 30, 1970," Alicia commented again.

I stared out the viewport and didn't dare pan to my wife. Note to self: Only sealed containers allowed in cockpit on future voyages. This scenario played out three more times before the panoramic view returned to something familiar.

Alicia guided the machine down into my backyard and initiated the shutdown sequence. The whirring of the propulsion system stopped, and the craft hovered above the ground.

"Shutdown sequence complete," said Alicia. "You may exit the vehicle, Chase."

"Thank you, Alicia," I said, before turning to my wife, who maintained her folded arms and death stare. "Alicia, transfer video and data to home server number one."

"Data transfer initiated," responded the AI voice. "Have a nice day, Chase."

"Thank you, Alicia," I said again.

The cockpit door opened, allowing us to leave. Jaime unbuckled herself, grabbed her dirty T-shirt, and swiveled out of her seat.

"I hate Alicia," she said, scrunching low to exit the craft. "Why don't you have someone like James Bond or Morgan Freeman talk to you?" From outside the vehicle, the tirade continued, "Don't forget your fucking soda, dumbass." A reasonable parting shot, I surmised.

After exiting the ship, I gazed at my digital wristwatch, then to the clock on my workbench. 12:34 PM. We arrived only a second after we left.

"Hey, we didn't come back a thousand years in the future!" I exclaimed. "I'll see you inside in a bit, I need to analyze some data," I continued, hoping for no answer. None came. I breathed a big sigh of relief. Note to self: Allow for configurable AI voice actors. Note to self, two: Keep Alicia as default.

Though we returned in one piece, and at the correct time, I still had a nagging feeling. Thus, the need to analyze the trip data. I went to my home office and logged onto my laptop. The craft's flight data waited for analysis. I opened the spreadsheet and started to gloss over the numbers.

"What?" I said, finding more than one anomaly. "This looks all wrong."

I followed the trail of timestamps starting from the beginning until the numbers eschewed. Then it hit me. The data changed when I spilled the soda. Dumbass, indeed. I examined the numbers more, finding five distinct occurrences of invalid results.

I sat back for a moment, allowing my brain to churn and digest the data. Opening another tab, I reviewed the diagnostic tests. Sure enough, things didn't add up. More unexpected results coincided with timestamps, times, and locations after the craft exited stealth mode. To make matters worse, the timestamps matched dates in the twentieth and twenty-first century.

"We must have skipped through time on our way home," I reasoned, putting the pieces together. Connecting the dots, I figured, "People might have seen us when our stealth capabilities went down."

Thinking hard, I pivoted to another stream of thought consciousness. I opened my Internet browser and entered the phrase "Unexplained dancing lights, South Africa, 1:37 PM, April 18, 1967" into the Google search bar. Sure enough, witnesses saw strange lights in the sky.

"That was me," I said.

I updated my search with the second set of parameters, "Unexplained dancing lights, Saunderstown, USA, 4:51 PM, March 30, 1970." Multiple groups of people reported a strange orb-shaped object darting across the sky above Narragansett Bay, then disappearing at a high rate of speed.

"Shit! That was me, too!"

"Unexplained dancing lights, Sicily, Italy, October 11, 2007." Fishermen witnessed a dancing orb zipping in the sky over their boats.

"Oh, boy!"

"Unexplained dancing lights, Sydney, Australia, 1:32 AM, June 2, 1995." A bright white orb zooming across the nighttime sky interrupted a teenage couple's romantic interlude.

"This can't be!"

"Unexplained dancing lights, Chile, South America, March 10, 2015." Passengers aboard LATAM Flight 1480 reported a strange white, spherical object outside the port side of their aircraft before it zipped away and disappeared.

"Oh, dear God!"

I sat back in my chair after my final search concluded, realizing that I had inadvertently become part of history's unexplained dancing lights phenomenon. Little did everyone know that the UFOs they saw were really a regular guy traipsing through time by mistake. I guess you could call me the most famous UFO time traveler in history. The Master of Dancing Lights, you might say.

I smiled. Not the worst title in the world. And, I built a time machine that works, even if I did need to clean up some sugary residue. Pretty remarkable if I say so myself. Not bad for a dumbass.

Mike Squatrito has been writing *The Overlords* series for over twenty years. He lives in Tiverton with his wife Lea and their dog Zoe. Mike speaks at schools, colleges, and libraries, to inspire everyone he meets to follow their dreams. He is the president of the Association of Rhode Island Authors (ARIA).

Active in sports, he is a knuckleball pitcher for the Narragansett Brewers (2008 and 2014 National Champions). He runs, does weight and cardio training, and takes yoga classes. Mike is an engineer by day, working on Homeland Defense projects.

Matters of the Heart
(Inspired by true events)

— *Barbara Ann Whitman*

Betsy stood by the mailbox in the morning sun and stared at the flyer for a long moment, a flurry of emotion stirring in her gut. "Annual Celebration of Life," it read. "Honoring donors, supporting families, and celebrating the lives of recipients." It had been eighteen months since the unthinkable had happened. She'd wished it had been her own heart that would soon stop beating instead of her grandson Justin's. There had been so much time by his bedside leading up to that point. She'd slept in the chair by his bed, praying for a miracle. When it became clear that one was not coming, she'd made the most heart-wrenching decision of her life. Once made, there were few precious moments remaining. The harvesting team was waiting to swoop in and carve up his young body. Betsy had imagined vultures circling above, rushing her last minutes with her only grandchild.

Then, the surgeon who would be recovering and preserving his organs asked Betsy to accompany Justin to the operating room. She'd not expected that. She agreed, if for no other reason than to postpone her inevitable final goodbye before his heart, lungs, kidneys, liver, and eyes would be surgically removed. She was completely unprepared for what happened next. The hospital corridor was lined with doctors, nurses, and other hospital staff, in solemn tribute to Justin's gift of life - and to Betsy's sacrifice. She later learned this was known as an Honor Walk. The final swell of pride she felt for her grandson gave some buoyancy to her pain, if only for those few moments.

Betsy tried so hard to focus on the good, to imagine the joy of another family whose loved one was being given a second chance because of Justin's untimely death. Sometimes she succeeded. Other times, she could not shake the vision of his final moments: the silencing of the beeping monitor, the confusing continued whoosh of the respirator that would pump oxygen to his body's organs until they were removed.

She considered the flyer again, tried to imagine herself attending, perhaps meeting others who had lived the same nightmare. *Would it help? Or only make the remembering worse?* She only allowed brief interludes with memories of that awful day, before distracting herself any way she could. Immersing herself in a weekend of reliving it seemed ghastly. Not to mention the idea of traveling halfway across the country by herself: that would be a first. Betsy went back inside, put the flyer down and decided to watch television for a while.

That night, she dreamed she was on a plane. Justin was in the seat beside her. He was whole and healthy, as he had been at 23, just before death. She looked at his handsome face, which always made her feel like she was looking at her son. Their profiles were almost identical. Justin turned to her and took her hand. He spoke in a soothing voice, encouraging her to do something that she felt reluctant about. Betsy awakened with a warm feeling which was quickly replaced by a stabbing sadness. A celestial visit from her grandson. The grief support group had taught her that. Initially, dreaming of Justin brought her to her knees in agony. It took time, but it was starting to work.

"What are you trying to say to me, Justin?" she asked the empty bedroom.

Shuffling to the kitchen, she put the kettle on. She reached for her favorite teacup, the well-used one with hearts around the rim that Justin had given her on her first Mother's Day as a grandmother. The pamphlet caught her eye from the pile of mail on the counter. *Hmmm. Is that what you're trying to tell me?*

Betsy took the flyer into the living room, along with her tea. On her tablet, she typed in the web address printed on the flyer, where it said, "For more information." She scrolled through images from past events: smiling faces gathered around a buffet table, hundreds of colorful balloons against a blue sky — a ceremonial release. An intimate group was gathered at a round table, listening to a speaker. The event was at a small midwestern college campus in summer, when guests could stay in the empty dorms. A bus would be ready to visit a memorial hall at the sponsoring agency's headquarters. Names of organ donors were engraved on bricks. There, flowers and other personal tributes lay.

Betsy closed the tablet. Her short "wallow window" closed with it. She'd impatiently hoped that, by now, her tolerance for dwelling on the matter would be easier, her grief less excruciating. She'd been wrong.

Justin was more than just her grandson. She'd raised him after his father died from cancer when Justin was just five. His mother had taken off years before, just disappeared. Postpartum depression was the public excuse, but Betsy had suspected drugs. Betsy had been widowed young, when Justin was thirteen. He had given her reason to get out of bed every morning. Then, ten years later, he left her, too.

She sipped her cooling tea as the rising sun warmed the room, shining on Justin's senior high school photo, framed on the end table. He had not changed much in the subsequent years, maintaining his boyish smile. He'd complained about having to take time to have the photo taken. "I'll miss basketball practice, Gam," he'd protested. She'd been Gam since he was a toddler

and he'd never called her anything else. She had shown him his dad's graduation picture, still displayed on the bookcase. "Pictures are all I have of your father," she told him. "Imagine if he'd been too stubborn to have this taken." Afterward, she felt bad about guilting Justin into the photo shoot. Little did she know that the treasured school picture would be his last formal photo.

Ringing jarred her from her thoughts. Her friend, Darlene, was smiling from the phone's screen.

"Hi, Bets! Hope I didn't wake you. How's it going?"

"Oh, okay, Darl. How are you?"

"Just okay?" she asked. "What's going on?"

Betsy knew better than to dodge the question. Darlene would get it out of her sooner or later. The two women had been friends since they were in high school themselves. Darl had seen her through all of life's celebrations and devastations. So she told her about the invitation to the Annual Celebration of Life and the dream of flying somewhere with Justin at her side.

"Oh, Bets. Are you considering this event? Do you really think you might go?"

"I don't know. Everything about it sounds like a bad idea. But the Universe is telling me to go."

"The Universe, huh?"

Betsy knew she hadn't heard the last of it.

* * *

It had been a few weeks since Betsy had been to the grief support group. The donor event had her spiraling. She could count on them to ask the right questions to help her decide about going. Checking her calendar, she saw that tomorrow was the second Thursday of the month, the day the group met in the church hall.

"Betsy!" A chorus of voices greeted her warmly as several members rushed to hug her. She was glad she'd come and felt reassured about seeking their help.

"We're so happy to see you!" said Marcia. Close to Betsy's age, she had lost her daughter in a house fire. Marcia now played a big role in her own grandson's life since his mother's death. She had been very sympathetic to learn that Betsy had raised Justin after losing her son.

Jack, who'd lost his wife and had recently taken up baking, handed Betsy a chocolate chip cookie wrapped in a napkin. "Get 'em while you can," he said, smiling. "I made them this afternoon and they're still warm!"

They made their way to folding chairs, arranged in a circle. Betsy saw that Cate still led the meetings. She had retired from a long career in social work and brought a sense of caring to the group, while keeping meetings structured and on track. Betsy listened to Cate's familiar soothing voice, moving from a confidentiality reminder to reading a poem by Ralph Waldo Emerson.

Cate surveyed the group. "Who would like to begin? Betsy, we haven't heard from you in a while…"

"Actually, I'd like some feedback about something," she began. The group listened attentively, nodding and murmuring occasionally. Betsy was encouraged and almost told them about the dream but thought better of it.

"Maybe you can call and get more information, so you'll know what to expect?" said Jack, kindly.

"Is there someone who might go with you that would be a source of support?" asked Marcia.

Betsy considered this. "I don't know…."

"A relative or a close friend?" asked another.

Cate spoke next. "Are you thinking that meeting other families of donors will be helpful to you? How would you feel to meet recipients of donated organs?"

Betsy froze. She had been so caught up in the fear of traveling alone and imagining walking into a room filled with strangers, she had not gotten any further in her thought process.

"Maybe I'm focused on the wrong things. I can't seem to get past the mechanics of getting there." She suddenly felt a little foolish.

Cate asked, "Is there someone who could help you with making reservations for flights, a rental car?"

"I could ask my friend, Darlene. She's pretty good with online stuff. And she travels some. More than I do, at least."

"That sounds like a good place to start," Cate said. "Once that's off your plate, you can focus on the actual event and what you hope to gain from attending."

Betsy felt more confident already. "Yes, I'll talk to Darlene tomorrow and ask her to show me how to book a flight. And I'll get more information about the conference itself and report back next month."

Jack raised his hand. "If your friend can't help, my daughter-in-law is the technology librarian in town here. I'm sure she'd be willing to show you."

"Thank you, Jack, and everyone. I knew I'd come to the right place."

* * *

Darlene sat beside Betsy on the couch, her laptop open between them. She expertly typed in some keywords and demonstrated how to scroll through the various airlines and flights, comparing times and prices. Betsy was intrigued and admired her friend's ease with the whole process.

"You now," Darlene began cautiously. "If it would make things easier for you, I'd be happy to go with you. Unless it's something you need to face alone. But, you'd have company and we could find something else to do or just head home early. I could leave the return flight open ended!"

"Oh, Darl. I don't know. That's awfully generous of you. But it all feels so monumental. I hate to ask you to do that."

"Well, you think about it. The offer stands, if it would help."

"The only thing that would help right about now is a glass of wine. Shall we?"

* * *

"I've made a decision," Betsy told the support group, four weeks later. "I'm going to the donor event!" There was a small round of light applause and smiles of approval. "My best friend, Darlene, is coming with me. We leave Sunday." 5.

"Good for you!" said Marcia. Sitting beside her, Jack raised a cookie, as if making a toast.

Cate asked, "Can you share any details you've learned about the event?"

"Yes. There's a meet-and-greet the first night for newcomers. I talked to the nicest woman on the phone and she sent me an itinerary. She said everything is optional. I can do as much or as little as I feel comfortable doing. The program speakers are all family members of organ donors, too, so there will be a lot of support."

"You seem happy with your decision," Cate said. "Maybe you'll share some stories with us next time."

* * *

The three-hour flight was difficult. Justin had been Betsy's only travel companion in recent years, and she missed him so terribly that she could hardly breathe at times. She wondered again if these moments were ever going to get easier. Darlene had buried her face in a book before takeoff and remained there until the pilot announced that landing was imminent. Betsy was tired when their Uber dropped them at the college. Registration was well organized, and the two women were escorted to the double dorm room they'd be sharing for the next two nights. The newcomer meet-and-greet would be in an hour, followed by dinner. Betsy wanted to unpack and relax.

Darlene was rummaging through her suitcase. "Voila!" she said exuberantly. Betsy turned to find her friend hoisting a bottle of merlot, which she promptly placed on the desk, beside the hotel-style ice bucket and water glasses provided. She caught Betsy's look, a mix of surprise and concern. "We are on a college campus, after all," she said, giggling.

Betsy rolled her eyes but agreed to half a glass. She wasn't much of a drinker and the gesture felt frivolous for such a somber event. She brightened when Darlene offered up a toast. "To the bravest woman I know. Here's to facing life: the good, the bad, and the downright ugly."

Betsy raised her glass in return. "And to good friends who stand by through it all." She was very glad to have Darl by her side.

* * *

The meet-and-greet was low-key and casual, much to Betsy's relief. She introduced herself to the facilitator, the very woman she'd spoken to on the telephone. "Welcome! I'm so glad you decided to join us. Tonight and tomorrow will be only for families of donors, so everyone has a unique, but shared journey. The final day will include some of our recipients and a ceremony to celebrate their lives, which were made possible by all of you."

She wasn't sure how to react but the woman seemed to understand, placing a hand on her arm.

"Take it one step at a time and feel free to step out if you need a break. I know it can be a lot. We've all been there."

After a short welcome speech, the donor family members were given photo IDs to hang around their necks as well as campus maps and the three-day itinerary. Darlene was given a visitor badge with her name and designating her as a support person.

Dinner followed and by the time dessert was served, Betsy was wiped out. "Travel doesn't agree with me," she told Darlene. "I'm exhausted already!"

"Probably a combination of the adrenalin leaving your body, now that you're actually here, and the high emotions you must be feeling. Let's make it an early night so you'll be rested for tomorrow."

* * *

After a quick nightcap, the women retired to their surprisingly comfortable twin beds. Darlene read for a while, but Betsy announced that she was too tired. She felt reassured by her friend's presence. But more than that, she felt Justin was present somehow, too. She was sleeping in no time.

In her dreams, she saw her grandson from a distance. Again, he was whole and healthy. She walked toward him and he turned to her, smiling and opening his arms. Betsy fell into him, and he hugged her tightly. Her ear was pressed against his chest and the sound of his beating heart erased all of the angst she'd been carrying since his death. She awakened slowly, tears of joy still wet on her face. Betsy hoped Darlene hadn't heard her and she was relieved that all was dark and silent on that side of the room.

Over breakfast, they studied the day's offerings. There were support groups, craft workshops for things called Memory Boxes and Luminaries. There was even a blood drive and a nature hike.

"I think the morning hike sounds nice," Betsy said. "It might help clear the cobwebs and put me in a good place for the rest." She recounted the dream for Darlene, hoping to shake it off and put it in perspective.

"You know," Darlene began. "They say that you dream of one of two things: something you fear will happen or something you hope will happen."

Betsy thought for a moment. "Well, I certainly would love for it to happen, but that's impossible."

* * *

"Perfect weather for a hike!" a woman walking near her said. Betsy agreed. Mostly, she was relieved. Everyone was friendly, offering a smile or greeting, but there were no uncomfortable disclosures or personal questions. Everyone appeared to either be lost in thought or immersed in nature. Betsy decided they were working on their own grief. She tried to do the same, uttering a small prayer of thanks that the others were respecting her privacy. Betsy was able to relax and enjoy the activity. She took a deep breath and felt at ease; her shoulders relaxed. She made a mental note to walk more, once she returned home. It was a far better distraction than television, when her thoughts ran dark.

Back inside the college center, she found Darlene. "Look what I made for tonight!" she exclaimed proudly. "It's a Luminaria. We're going to line the driveway after dark and light them." It was a beautifully decorated bag of some sort of heavy paper with a battery-operated candle inside. Darlene had painted a skateboard on one side, with Justin's name on it. On the other side she had drawn a horse, surrounded by a sky filled with stars.

"I don't know what to say," Betsy said through teary eyes. "It's beautiful. And it's so Justin." She hugged her friend. Lost in her own grief, she often forgot that Darlene missed Justin, too. She had always been "Aunt" Darlene. She had taken Justin horseback riding for the very first time when he was six. He had loved it, almost as much as skateboarding.

The rest of the day flew by, and the two women caught up again before dinner. Darlene had attended a presentation about passion fatigue, where she shared her insights with Betsy, who had been busy learning the range of things that could come next for her. Many people were further along in their journeys, and some had become ambassadors for organ donation, helping to educate the public. "I'm not saying I'm ready for anything like that yet, but I could see myself becoming some sort of advocate in the future."

"I'm happy to hear you're looking forward," Darlene said. "You sound hopeful for the first time in a long time."

"Nineteen months," Betsy said. "But who's counting?" She smiled.

* * *

During dinner, there was a speaker who talked about "the other side." She explained what the donation process was like for those receiving organs, as well as their families. She said she hoped to ease the anticipation they were bound to be feeling about meeting recipients at tomorrow's events. While many donors and recipients chose anonymity, some mutually chose to establish contact. A panel of organ recipients would be speaking during their final breakfast together and then answering questions.

"That sounds amazing," Darlene said cautiously. "I remember how you struggled with the decision not to hear from recipients of Justin's organs."

"At the time, I couldn't wrap my head around it. Now I sometimes wonder if I made the right choice."

Darlene waited for more, but Betsy changed the subject. "I hoped to squeeze in a visit to the Memorial Hall. I wasn't sure I'd be up for that, either – seeing Justin's name engraved and all. But now that I'm here, I need to go."

"The shuttles run every hour," Darlene said, studying the itinerary. "Can we get there and back between breakfast and the farewell lunch?"

"Let's do it!" Besty said. "We'll leave right after the presentation."

* * *

Betsy looked serious throughout the morning talk, as if weighing every word. "Are you okay?" Darlene asked.

"It's a lot to process. I remember holding my pen over the unchecked box allowing recipients to contact me. I just wasn't in a good place to be making that kind of decision. Now I wonder… Maybe I should have checked that box."

"Maybe you can still do it," Darlene suggested. "You know – amend your original contract?"

The presentation ended and the women made a beeline to the shuttle stop. Thirty minutes later, they arrived at the Memorial Hall. Although a brightly lit and comfortable room, the atmosphere was one of somber respect. Darlene ran her finger down a posted list of donor's names that included their locations on the four walls of engraved bricks. "Found him," she said. "Row E, line 26."

Betsy scanned the rows, looking at the mementos left by loved ones – pictures, wilting flowers, small personal items. She sucked in her breath when she saw Justin's name. His brick was shiny and unblemished, one of the newer ones. She gently traced each letter with her fingers. Darlene stood close by, moving near enough to place a hand around Betsy's waist when her friend's shoulders began to shake.

"I didn't think to bring anything," Betsy said. She opened her pocketbook and withdrew her wallet. Justin's smile peeked out and she carefully slid it from the plastic sleeve. "His graduation picture," she said with a hint of pride.

Darlene found a basket filled with tape, scissors, and other items. Together, they affixed the photo to the wood framing the brick. Betsy stood back and smiled through her tears. "That's better." She kissed her fingertips and touched Justin's face.

* * *

"Oh no! Look at the time!" Betsy cried. Hurrying to the shuttle stop, they watched as it pulled away without them. "Now we'll miss the last session - and lunch!" She plopped down on a wooden bench. Darlene followed.

"You could go back inside and spend more time in the hall," Darlene offered.

"That's okay. It's just a brick. I don't know why I was so afraid!" Betsy shrugged.

After some time had passed in silence, a few others joined them to wait, taking the bench opposite the two women. Polite hellos were exchanged. They compared notes about the conference, passing the time amicably.

Betsy studied the young man sitting across from her. There was something very familiar about him. Had he been a member of the panel of organ recipients that spoke at breakfast?

"Is this your first time here?" he asked politely.

Here we go, she thought. *The personal information I'd hoped to avoid.* "Yes," she said.

"Are you a donor family or recipient?"

119

"Donor," Betsy said. "My grandson." She looked down, fearing the tears she felt building behind her eyes might spill and give her away.

"Thank you," he said sincerely. "I owe my life to families like yours."

The kid has a lot of nerve, was Betsy's initial thought. But he seemed genuine. Darlene started to say something, but Betsy held up a hand. "It's okay, Darl." She was surprised at her own willingness to answer him. She looked at her feet, allowing a few tears to fall. "Maybe it's time I talked about Justin."

"Do you know any of Justin's recipients?" he asked.

"No," Betsy said. "I opted not to, at the time. Now I'm beginning to regret my decision, especially after hearing from the panel this morning." She hoped he'd confirm that's why she felt connected to this young man, who couldn't have been much older than Justin when he died.

"I get it - it must be such a painful time. I think that's why my donor family never reached out."

"My name is Michael, by the way. I'm from New York."

"We're from Massachusetts," Betsy said.

"I know Massachusetts! I received my new heart at Mass General," Michael said. "I love Boston."

Betsy raised her eyes to meet his. "When was that?" she asked, her voice shaking.

"May 30th, exactly nineteen months ago. My donor died from a head injury when he was thrown from his horse. We were the same age, twenty-three."

It took a moment for Betsy to find her voice. "Justin was twenty-three."

Betsy heard Darlene's breath catch.

"Oh my God," was all Betsy could say. It came out in a whisper. "You have my Justin's heart," she finally managed. "You have my grandson's heart."

Michael stood and opened his arms. Betsy fell into them, and he hugged her for a long time. Betsy pressed her ear against his chest and listened to his beating heart.

Barbara Ann Whitman's work has been published in all ten ARIA anthologies. Her writing falls across many genres, including YA fiction, nonfiction, short stories and poetry. She is a seasoned social worker whose career has transcended generations of diverse individuals and families, from newborn to geriatric. Her novel, *Have Mercy*, was inspired by her years in child protection. "Matters of the Heart" was inspired by an extraordinary story she heard years ago, from a treasured colleague.

Hymn to the Elixir Extraordinaire

— Risa Nyman

The figure form is cruel curse or brilliant blessing,
Perhaps you luxuriate in kudos or are beaten by taunts.
There's a season to be proud and a time for humiliation.

When the scale screams and shatters, voyeurs are birthed
To saunter and snicker at your every mouthful.
You become a craven creature, dining out on your own pity.

[*Gigantic sundae and plate towering with donuts. People tsking and lamenting audibly.*]

But behold, a sweet savior appears in a tube of magic.
With a fabulous juice only for the chosen,
Those invited into the mystery of transcendent transformation.

Embarrassing blubber evaporates, bulge-by-bulge.
Ages of amassed adipose succumb to this extraordinary elixir.
Hurrah to the mighty Oz! Hail to the great god of Thin!

[*Exaggerated genuflect at altar with pen-like tube displayed.*]

This splendiferous drug slingshots you to stardom,
Alters the body, creating a slender, superior soul.
Envy flows to the vaunted imbibers of this costly concoction.

The one-percenters, the sought-after, the nearly-famous
Sport a squinty mock on those unworthy of receiving the miracle,
Who are left doomed to descend into their whipped cream.

[*Waddling in circles with pillows strapped to belly. Loud heaving sighs…*]

The marvelous deep soak in their lies of sweaty work and measured morsels.
Gorging on frosted applause and accolade custards.
For almost godlike they are, demanding honor and homage.

Ah, but secrets will spill. Their masks will melt as faces fall, long and lined.
Shocked at their re-sculpting, exposing jutting chin and knobby knees.
Their naked cheat now revealed, shining in newly hollow, sunken eyes.

[*Claps of thunder. Sit facing audience with blackened eyes, pale white skin.*]

Risa Nyman recently returned to writing poetry to express what's closest to her heart and in the forefront of her mind. Her poem, "A Father's Advice," appeared in the 2023 ARIA anthology *In a Dark Time*. She has written middle grade mysteries and a young adult novel, published by Immortal Works Press.

The Orphanage of Damocles

—Steven R. Porter

My fingers now tremble so uncontrollably I can no longer grip my beloved cup of tea. My bedroom is dark as death, yet I dare not switch on a lamp. I find comfort in shadows these days for fear that even a single sliver of light will force me to gaze upon the horror of what I have created and prove my darkest fears true.

I am unable to allow myself the comfort of even a moment of relaxation. The chanting never ends. Often it starts with gentle whispers that arise from the basement and only become louder as I grind my palms into my ears, praying for the torture to cease. But it's the moaning that is most horrifying and causes my throat to clench and breath to forsake me. I can feel their anger radiate through the floor and into the soles of my sore, arthritic feet. They know I am here. They know it was me. They will not let me forget.

I regret everything I have done and would sacrifice my own decrepit life to undo it all if I could. Was I mad then...or am I mad now? I fear my mind has become far too broken to know the difference.

So please, before my pathetic world comes to an end and I am mercifully assigned to the depths of hell, allow me the decency of a proper confession.

It all began with the purest of intentions, I swear to almighty God, with an innocent visit to a used bookstore. One morning, I spied a discarded advertising circular floating in a mud puddle outside my home. It read, in part:

Damocles Books
Thousands of Great Used Titles as Low as One Dollar.

Bespectacled quasi-intellectuals such as I can't resist the lure of a true used bookshop. How could I have not heard about this place before now? I felt a sudden rush of adrenaline ripple through my veins. Pure joy. An afternoon spent floating among the stacks to find hidden treasure always made me feel like a prospector working a field to unearth a long-lost nugget of gold. It would be like an afternoon among new friends. Since my retirement from the university where I labored as an archivist for the academic library, I had grown quite lonely. Human friends in my world are few and far between, and having never married, I might go a week or more without any type of formal social interaction. My personal book collection, of course, became my steadfast loyal companion. And there was always room for another volume to find itself upon my bookshelf of close personal friends.

The shop was a challenge to find, nestled within the dusty bowels of an old, abandoned New England textile mill. It was packed to the rafters with thousands of discarded tomes, each once part of someone's personal collection. The brick outer walls of the mill were cracked in too many places to count. Moisture, the one true enemy of any book, was evident everywhere through leaks in the mortar or from multiple patches of mildew smeared upon many of the cheap brown laminated bookshelves that attempted to keep the collection organized. A large steel industrial fan circulated heavy musty air around the space. The smooth, greasy, antique floorboards creaked with every step, no doubt intended to alert any bookseller in earshot of a wandering customer's presence.

Despite the utter joy that consumed me, I could sense something was not quite right. There was a specter of sadness and anxiety that hung above the collection like a bank of pea soup fog. I could not explain it. Did all those years entombed in the depths of the academic library give me some supernatural insight? Ignore it, I convinced myself. Why allow a bout of childish paranoia to spoil a damned good thing?

The proprietor of the shop was an odd fellow named Curwen. He was a round man with a protruding belly and long, bluish-white beard. As I wandered from room to room and aisle to aisle in his shop, he would be dutifully classifying and shelving new arrivals as if I were not there, and only looked up from his work when I approached the cash register, wiggling my leather wallet in the air.

I got to know old Curwen quite well over that fateful summer. He wore the same threadbare green woolen sweater and tan corduroy trousers every day, yet did not appear to draw any embarrassment from doing so. I made dozens of visits to his shop, each time rescuing an old volume of poetry or some obscure Victorian novel from his collection. It got so that I am convinced I knew the store's inventory better than Curwen himself. I was continually amazed at the depth of selection his hole-in-the-wall bookstore offered. My background as an archivist, coupled with my exceptional memory, allowed me to close my eyes and visualize the spines of the books that lined his shelves. And I could visualize them all as I dozed off to sleep each night. Of course, anytime Curwen placed a newly acquired volume in its rightful place, I would notice immediately.

It took a few months, but I am embarrassed to admit I became bored with the place. I needed more volumes to feed my growing appetite. New books were not arriving fast enough to satisfy my craving. Even old Curwen would roll his bloodshot eyes at the mere sight of me strolling through the door each afternoon. I don't think he liked me very much, but that was okay, since he had never been the object of my interest. As long as the door was unlocked when I arrived and books remained in their proper place, I felt obliged to be there, Curwen be damned. I took particular care to be sure to handle every volume on each shelf in an outrageous act of thoroughness – I needed to know them all. I didn't understand why. Just not yet anyway.

It was then that my superior observational skills focused on a brown door in the corner. It felt as if something behind it was calling out to me. Could this be the source of my obsession with the place? It must be! I could on occasion hear faint whispers and rhythmic mumbles as if someone was chanting an obscure mantra. The door was blocked by a three-legged wooden chair, an empty pizza box, and a few grimy plastic shipping containers.

"This door," I asked Curwen, who looked at me over the top of a thick cookbook with a sneer of profound annoyance, "I walk by it every time I visit. It intrigues me. You must tell me what's behind it."

"Nothing!" he replied curtly. Curwen could never be accused of being an adept conversationalist. "Damaged books. Old boxes. Trash. That's about it. Mostly things that need to go to the dump."

"Do you mind?" I asked as my hand was thrust forward for the door handle, my chubby fingers wiggling with curious anticipation.

"Wait! In fact, yes. I do mind. What's in that room is not of anyone's concern but mine and mine alone," he said with a tenor of disdain to his voice, folding his meaty, freckled arms across his chest.

Curwen had never been overtly rude before, and his unanticipated grouchiness only fueled my interest. Oh, how I love a good mystery! He was clearly hiding something, something wondrous I deduced. Could there be discarded books of immense value? Manuscripts? Ephemera? Perhaps something rare? Could whatever exists behind that door satisfy my lust? Oh, how I had to know!

I did not need to wait long to find out. After Curwin's abrupt dismissal, I wandered off and tried to lose myself in an aisle of paperback science fiction novels. I spend far too much time here on typical days and figured I would make myself invisible and simply blend into the stacks. Curwen would eventually forget I was here as he was prone to do. I was also aware old Curwen was afflicted with an embarrassing medical issue many men face in their waning years, and I only had to be patient before he tottered off to the restroom to address his misery. His exodus on that fateful afternoon happened even sooner than I had hoped.

The moment I heard the last floorboard creak beneath Curwen's brown loafers, and the restroom latch clank behind him, I made a beeline for that mysterious door. The debris that blocked my path was no deterrence as it was easily swept away with a simple backhand. I could hear the murmurs, whispers, and moans with much more clarity though I still could not decipher their meaning. There was no lock, so the tarnished brass doorknob turned with ease, nearly falling off in my palm. I stood frozen at the threshold squinting into the darkness. The rhythmic chants sounded Gregorian in nature and familiar, though I could not place them.

I stepped inside to the most bizarre of scenes. The room, which reeked of incense, was small, double the size of a typical broom closet, with no windows or light fixtures of any sort. Yet, originating from the center of the room was the source of those sounds; an eerie glow illuminated the space just enough for my mortal eyes to see.

And oh, what a sight it was! This was no room filled with trash; it was treasure. I was right to believe that Curwin was a fraud! A single book lay open on a mahogany end table. Its pages were ornamented in silver and gold trim while its pages gleamed with bright red letters. Despite my advanced education, I could not verify the language, but it was evident that it was ancient and rare. My hands trembled. My spine tingled. It was by far the most extraordinary volume I had ever encountered. I was driven to touch it, to embrace it… to consume it.

I reached forward and rubbed the page tenderly with the back of my hand as one might stroke the cheek of a lover, when without warning, the room exploded in crashing waves of sound. I instinctively covered my ears, but it was of no use. The noise easily permeated through the aged flesh of my fingers, violating my eardrums. It was those whispers I had been hearing – it was no chant but the amplified agony of thousands of voices all shouting at once!

I fell to my knees, still cupping my ears. Through the cacophony and my misery, I could hear individual voices and slowly came to the cold realization of who was shouting. It was the books themselves! I crawled into the corner of the closet and tried to make myself as small as possible in the hopes that whoever was causing this would forget I was there. But I would not be granted any such mercy.

Help me!

Return me to my library!

Please, please! My owner. We must find her. She is not well.

Take me home!

Someone… save me from this terrible place!

It took some time, but through the seemingly impenetrable noise, I was able to isolate individual voices that would tell me their stories. One book told of the horror of being left in a box on the side of the road. Another spoke of being nearly shredded by dozens of shoppers at a library book sale. And another mourned their owner's death and how the beloved collection of which they were a part was dispersed by the woman's children. I came to realize that my ordinary bookshop was more like an orphanage that housed thousands of terrified, abandoned, leatherbound children looking to be reclaimed and loved.

I do not know to this day whether I fell asleep in that corner or passed out from the chaos around me. I awoke several hours later and struggled to straighten my arthritic back and get to my feet. The noise that reverberated in my skull had not abated, and I knew that I needed to get out, to save my sanity and perhaps even my life. I pushed the closet door open with my index finger and scanned the aisles for any sign of old Curwen, but the lights had been turned off and it was difficult to see. According to my wristwatch, it was three in the morning. Did Curwen not know I was here and locked the place up for the night?

I walked across the creaking wooden floorboards, slipped through the front door, and a few moments later found myself standing alone on a crumbling sidewalk. The voices had not subsided at all, and the mile-long trek back to my home was torturous. I had assumed distance from the horror would restore my senses, but I could not have been more wrong. The voices, the begging, and the pleas tortured my every step.

Save me. Save me.

Days passed, or perhaps it was weeks. It was hard to tell as I tossed and turned upon my bed, drifting in and out of consciousness. The voices from those books forced my perceptions to spiral into a place so dark I can't bring myself to describe it. I tried to numb myself with inebriation, but even drunkenness served to only amplify my sorry state. Those parts of my mind that maintained my sanity struggled to find a solution and reached one terrible conclusion. To save my miserable life, that beautiful, glowing, extraordinary, evil book needed to be destroyed.

With all the energy I could muster, I exhumed my brittle, shivering body from my bed and dragged it back down the street to the bookstore. The hour was approaching midnight. The moonlight helped illuminate my way, but as helpful as the moonlight was, I worried it might reveal my questionable intentions to anyone who might be passing by. I was able to snap a rusty latch off the back door near the fire escape with ease to gain entry. Inside the shop, the books were all aligned in their rightful spots as you might expect, bathed by the darkness, in what most would describe as an eerie silence. It was a scene I would have enjoyed had it not been for the incessant clamoring in my head.

I opened the closet door, and oh yes…there it was. The most beautiful book I had ever seen illuminated the room with a warm, pulsating amber glow. My heart fluttered in my chest as I approached. My fingertips tingled. I was conflicted. Despite the torment it bestowed upon me, driving me to the brink of madness, I still wanted to save it. Protect it. I stroked it with tenderness and felt tears well-up in the corner of my eyes. I took a deep breath and struck a wooden match against the side of my matchbox.

At first, even the lit match appeared confused. The flame stood tall between my thumb and index finger, and I swear it looked at me as if to ask, *are you sure this is what do you want me to do? Here? Now?*

I hesitated. And in my stupor, I didn't notice that a tiny piece of the matchhead had broken off and landed on the floor between my shoes. So many of these old New England mills have been around for two hundred years. And through most of their existence, the machinery that was housed within them leaked all sorts of oils and nasty flammable lubricants, soaking the wooden floorboards. With thousands of volumes of paper stored within its walls, the mill could now only be described as an ideal funeral pyre.

All around me the floor took to flame and spread with astonishing speed. I looked around for some way to douse what I had created, but there was nothing at hand other than a crusty dry mop and a rusty bucket. I tried to stomp out the fire but to no avail. My head jerked from side to side, and I began to hyperventilate when I was startled by a wisp of acrid, smoky air that filled my lungs. Survival instincts took over. It was then I knew I needed to escape before the doorway succumbed to the inferno, trapping me there inside, sealing my fate.

By the time I stumbled my way through the closet door, across the shop, and found myself out in the street, the building had become fully engulfed. I stood frozen in horror as I watched the flames curl upwards, dancing in and out of the mill's windows. I could not bear to look away. The voices in my head had gone silent, but the wondrous relief I had been craving was momentary. All those voices that had been the bane of my existence for weeks were replaced by a voice screaming in agony – but this time it was just one and it was muffled. Yet this one I recognized – it was Curwen! How could I possibly know he lived in an apartment on the floor above the bookshop! I looked up and saw him pounding on his window, eyes wide and mouth open, gasping for breath, his face melting with an unforgettable ghoulish look of terror. Before I could even consider my options, he slipped down and out of sight in a horrific cyclone of smoke and flame.

Dear God, what had I done?

I leaned against a telephone pole near the street corner to cough, vomit, and regain my senses when I first heard the sirens. Big red trucks seemed to fly in from every direction. There were a dozen of them by daybreak. I sat on a swing in an adjacent playground to consider the colossal horror I had created, and watch as a small army of men risked their lives to extinguish it. The mill was a total loss. The books were ash. Curwen was gone.

Exhausted, I slogged my way home, longing to hide beneath the safety of my blankets. Perhaps after some sleep, I thought, I would wake up to learn it had all been a horrible nightmare. I had barely moved across the threshold of my house when the voices in my head returned. But this time there were no pleas or requests for help, only accusations.

Murderer.

Killer.

Arsonist.

Criminal.

Thief.

In all the chaos, it never occurred to me that by removing the beautiful, exotic, mysterious book from the shop and saving it from becoming ash, its mystical powers would penetrate my own beloved book collection here in my own home. Now, as I cradled the beautiful book in my arms, I listened as my most dear friends all turned against me.

In a fit of rage, I grabbed them all, armload by armload, and threw them into the cellar. Who are they to question my honor! They did not understand what I had been through. Ingrates! I could feel all their moans and screams as they bounced one stair to the next, ricocheting off walls, and slamming into the cold concrete floor, pages torn and spines broken. But what did I care. I had the one book that mattered. It is the only book I would need for the rest of my life.

So that is my story. I regret it all. Shower me with indifference or pity if you must, it matters not to me any longer. I have lived in this self-imposed hell now for six months with barely any food or sleep and do not possess the will to break from it. My body is succumbing. I know I will be dead soon to the delight, I presume, of my personal library, which continues its relentless torment of my sanity. But if there is any solace in what remains of my existence, it is that by recounting my story, it will become mystically absorbed into the one book that has not left my arms since that fateful night. And to whoever shall inherit it after my passing, be forewarned that its pages will bear not only my tale, but the weight of my torment, as it lies in wait for a new soul to claim.

Steven R. Porter has written three novels: *Fiddlehead, Confessions of the Meek & the Valiant* and *Manisses,* and he is the co-author of *Scared to Death... Do it Anyway* about overcoming panic attacks. He owns Stillwater River Publications and Stillwater Books. He is founder of the Association of RI Authors.

Amour: a villanelle

— Kristen M. Castrataro

One with the breeze, the rye-grass flows
In undulating mounds of blue.
Is this the way in which love grows?

Does one the melody compose;
The other play their notes on cue?
One with the breeze, the rye-grass flows.

Or do they skirmish—friendly foes—
One another to subdue?
Is this the way in which love grows?

Is theirs a game like Manny Machado's,
Where each who caught then turned and threw?
One with the breeze, the rye-grass flows.

Can we who've suffered passion's blows
Grow strong and wise, pursue anew?
Is this the way in which love grows?

When we our pride and fear forgo

And live as one who once were two,
One with the breeze, the rye-grass flows:
This is the way in which love grows.

Kristen M. Castrataro helps people harness words to foster self-expression, emotional healing, and community. She is a certified Journal to the Self® instructor, the founder of Pen Light, LLC, and the author of two books, *Grandpa's Farm has LOTS of Saws* and *Whirring Wings: Songs from the Locust Years.*

Shredding the Veil:
an Encounter with a Feline Visitant

— Deborah Barchi

I once lived with a very special cat. I originally called him Paws because of the four bright spots of white on the paws of his otherwise all-black fur. As the months went by, I started to call him Kookieboy because of his bizarre, erratic, exasperating, and totally endearing behavior.

Kookieboy spent most of his life as an indoor/outdoor cat, with the emphasis on outdoor. Sometimes he spent all day and most of the night outdoors, roaming his territory, chasing off other cats, hunting mice and chipmunks. But if the weather was bad, or he was just in the mood for some companionship or uninterrupted sleep, he would come to my back door, demanding to be let in.

I loved the evenings when Kookieboy would decide to come sleep on my bed, especially on cold winter nights when the wind rattled the windows, owls called from the woods, and coyotes yipped and howled, seemingly right in front of the house.

Kookieboy would jump soundlessly from the bedroom floor to my bed, land on the quilted coverlet with a muffled thump, knead the quilt a few times, curl up and lean against my left knee, purr for a few moments, and sleep the night way.

For a cat who spent so much time outdoors, Kookieboy lived a very long life. He had surpassed his twentieth year when old age finally claimed him, quite peacefully one day in early autumn. With the help of my son, I wrapped his body in a fluffy towel, shrouded the towel in several plastic bags along with several of his favorite indoor toys, and buried him deep beneath a young copper beech tree I had planted only the year before.

I cried a little at the burial, but I didn't feel overwhelmed by grief. "Death comes to all things," I stoically reminded myself as the day wore on. But when I got into bed that night, grief for my sweet little cat suddenly overwhelmed me. I cried and cried and finally fell asleep many hours later, probably in the middle of a sob.

The next day I awoke, feeling a great hollowness in my chest. My eyes stung from all the tears I had shed during the night. Tears threatened all day, although I did all I could to suppress them during work hours. Each night I tossed and turned, unwilling to stop thinking of Kookieboy, almost as if by continuing to think of him, I might be keeping him alive.

"Why not get another cat?" friends and family urged. But I couldn't bear to think of such a disloyal act. For that's what it seemed to me, sentimental and unreasonable as it may have seemed to others.

About a week after Kookieboy died, I once again climbed into bed, exhausted from my sadness and from my erratic sleep of the past seven days. I lay on my back with my eyes tightly closed, willing sleep to come, knowing it would not, for many hours.

The curtains were drawn. The bedroom was in darkness. The only sounds were the hypnotic humming of the refrigerator in the kitchen and the occasional slight creaking of a floorboard in the attic.

Suddenly, unmistakably, I heard the muffled thump of a small creature landing on the bed. I felt it knead the coverlet a few times. I felt it (yes, unmistakably felt it) curl up and press against my left knee, purr so very quietly, and grow silent.

I felt two very distinct, warring feelings overpower my mind. One was terror for such an inexplicable, even ghostly encounter. The other was joy that my beloved cat had returned to me, somehow. Both feelings were intense and at war with each other for what seemed like an eternity, but probably only took a few moments.

One thing I knew for sure was that I was fully awake. I was not dreaming, not even a lucid dream. I was awake, and this extraordinary experience was happening.

I thought of sitting up and reaching out to pet the cat sleeping against my leg. But something, whether unreasoning terror or immense gratitude for this mysterious visitation, kept me from doing that. I felt that a wonderful mystery was balanced against scientific observation here. After a very short battle between my mind and my heart, I chose to accept the inexplicable experience as an act of humble faith.

I told no one of what happened. For two more nights, I waited to see if Kookieboy would return. He did. Each time my heart felt lighter and my mind slowly freed itself from its bitter grief. On wakening after the third night, I got up and went immediately to my computer to check on businesses that could make me a small grave marker I could place over the burial site for Kookieboy, under the copper beech tree.

I found a company that would make a custom inscription on pressed stone for a reasonable price, and deliver it within ten business days. I asked for the following inscription, including the affectionate words I would often murmur to Kookieboy as I greeted him each day:

Paws (aka Kookieboy)
1992-2012
The best little kitty cat in the world

I cried when I placed the stone above Kookieboy's gravesite. But they were no longer bitter tears. They felt more healing than hurtful. Something precious had passed from my life, but the memory of our warm companionship would always remain.

Not too long after I placed the stone over Kookieboy's grave, I decided I was ready to adopt another cat. I went to a local animal shelter and adopted not one, but two kittens, a brother and sister, the last remaining kittens from the same litter. That was almost twelve years ago, and Bruce, a handsome black cat, and his sister Bonnie, a pretty tortoiseshell, continue to be my sweet companions.

Thinking back on those three nights so many years ago, when Kookieboy jumped on my bed, and by his unexpected presence brought peace and acceptance to me regarding his passing from the earth, I know that there will be many who will smile knowingly and believe that I imagined or dreamed the whole thing. Nothing more extraordinary, they will think, than a very vivid dream brought on by my passionate emotion.

Everyone has the right to his or her own beliefs, of course. But I would just like to remind those folks of Hamlet's words to Horatio (Act 1, Scene 5) when Horatio expresses disbelief that Hamlet had encountered the ghost of his father):

"There are more things in heaven and earth, Horatio, than are dreamt of in your philosophy."

Deborah Barchi is a Rhode Island native living in Scituate. She is a retired librarian and published author who enjoys writing essays and poems about cats, nature, and childhood experiences, recollected through the lens of adulthood.

Curse of the Shellycoat

— Marie Ventura

"Mm!" April May took another huge bite of her spinach pie. She glanced up at her older brother, steam escaping her mouth as she spoke through the savory wad of spiced spinach, pepperoni, olives, and cheese. "'s good and hot. Come sit down, or I'll eat yours too!"

"In a minute." Julius adjusted his binoculars, taking a few steps closer to the icy tideline.

April grunted and munched the middle out of her spinach pie, then nibbled at the crunchy, chewy, cheesy crust.

The two teens had walked Barkley, their shaggy terrier, down the winding nature trail from the parking lot, braving sucking mud, bitter wind gusts, and eerie winter trees to picnic at Rome Point. April let the eager dog lick her hands 'clean,' then wiped her fingers on her jeans, standing to peer past her taller brother toward the rocky beach and rippling bay. A cluster of boulders poked up from the water, far enough out that her unaided eyes couldn't tell if the speck-small birds bobbing beside them were brants, gulls, or mergansers. Worse, zooming in with her phone turned the rocks and sparkling water into pixilated blurs.

"So..." She nudged her brother's arm. "Any seals out there today?"

Julius didn't lower the binoculars. "Eight or nine on the rocks. I think there's more in the water."

April kicked at the slipper shells the tides had piled among the sand and rocks and February frost. *Clatter. Clack.* She waited another long beat, then—

"You'll get your turn, okay?" Julius cut her off. "Quit bothering me!"

"Jerk. You're not the only one who wants to watch the seals." April shoved her empty take-out box into her backpack and sat on a fallen log, pulling her brother's box onto her lap, the food inside still warm despite the February wind. "I'm not kidding, you know," she warned. "I'm so starving, I really could eat yours."

"Wrrr*arf*!" Barkley wagged his tail.

April laughed and opened the box. "Here you go, Barkers. Have a piece of Julie's pepperoni."

"What – April!" Julius spun around and slapped the cardboard lid closed. "Seriously, keep your fingers out of my food!"

April smirked. "You didn't mind Amalthea Jones touching your spinach pie."

"Amalthea made them. It's her parents' pizza shop!" Julius brought the binoculars back to his eyes. "I can't figure it out. I've watched her – I know she follows her family's recipe to the letter. But, somehow, the pizzas and calzones she makes always taste better."

He tilted his head toward his sister without breaking his gaze through the binoculars. "Amalthea's the captain of your fencing team, right? She ever tell you her secret?"

"Hasn't come up. *Ooff.* But my spinach pie might."

April doubled over, clutching her stomach. Julius rolled his eyes.

"That's what you get when you inhale your food. We have teeth for a reason, you know."

"'s that how you plan to win the State Science Fair?" April snarked back. "Stating the obvious? *Ooh, I...*"

A low burble, warped and strange, sounded behind him, followed by the clatter of shells. Barkley barked and Julius sighed, his binoculars raised but his eyes closed.

"Come on, April." He turned to regard his little sister. "If you're gonna be sick, at least..."

He squinted, reflexively raising his hand against a sudden intense light.

"What the—! April?"

The flash faded quickly, but he didn't see his sister. Not on the log, not on the beach, not among the bare winter trees. Barkley whined and pawed at the clacking shells, but Julius grabbed his leash and pulled him away.

"April!" he shouted, stepping out into the wind. "April, this isn't funny! *APRIL!*"

***

"I searched literally everywhere!" Julius leaned over the window-like food guard separating Amalthea's ingredients from the customers at the counter. "Me and Barkley. I tried her phone – everything! April just, she vanished! *Oop!*"

His hand knocked against a Parmesan cheese shaker. Amalthea caught it before it splashed into the pool of sauce she'd just spread over a round of pizza dough.

"Whoa, good catch," he praised.

Amalthea set the shaker back in place. "You're not supposed to lean over the counter."

"Yeah, I know," he said, returning to his leaning position. Amalthea frowned until he straightened up.

"So, why do you do it?"

"I want to see how you make the pizzas," Julius told her. "But, Amalthea—"

"Aren't the police looking for her?" The teen sprinkled shredded cheese over the sauce, then started laying out pepperoni slices like playing cards.

Julius's expression darkened. "They say they are. But it's already been three days. And when that lieutenant guy talked to my parents…" He shook his head. "They don't know anything. Seriously, they think she's— But she's not! I know she's not! She's out there, Amalthea. Hurt or sick or I don't know what! That's why I need you to help me find her."

Amalthea sighed and reached for the mushrooms. "I'm not a detective, Julius."

"No, but you are, hands down, the smartest kid in our class. Probably the whole school.'

She lowered her eyes. "I'm good at solving word problems. *Fictional* mysteries. This is real life. And your sister. She's one of the best new fencers on the team. If, if I can't find her – or, if we do find her and she's, like—"

The bell over the entrance jangled and a cluster of uniformed cheerleaders poured in. Julius stepped aside to make room at the narrow counter, only to find his back pressed against the painted brick wall.

"Guess Saturday practice just got out."

Amalthea handled the noisy influx with unflappable calm, taking orders and names. As the squad scattered among the little pizzeria's narrow booths and tables to wait for their food, Julius couldn't help overhearing their conversation.

"No, it's true!" Josh, the team's top gymnast, held out his phone so the girls at his table could see the screen. "They're saying it's a new local cryptid – like the Mothman, in West Virginia."

"You can't see anything in that video," Marissa complained from another table. "Just a pile of blurry shells."

"But that's the thing – the creature is literally *made* of shells," Annie told her. "In dance class, they were saying it's like that old Irish legend of…um…the Shellycoat! That's what they're calling it!"

Amalthea skillfully shifted a steaming pizza from the scorching oven to a cardboard box, glancing at Julius as she cut it into slices. "What are they talking about?"

He tightened his jaw. "Some dumb video that's been going around. They're saying April disappeared because of this weird sea monster people claim they've seen stalking the shoreline."

Amalthea wrinkled her nose. "You can't be serious. Why do people always jump to supernatural stories when something weird happens?"

"You saying you don't believe in the Curse of the Shellycoat?" Julius raised a teasing eyebrow.

"I'm saying I doubt your sister got eaten by a storybook bogeyman." Amalthea stacked two more pizza boxes on the counter, then pushed a button on the wall that looked a lot like a doorbell. "Dad's turn on delivery duty," she explained, gesturing toward her family's upstairs apartment before shoving the cheerleaders' newly ordered pizzas and calzones into the oven.

Julius regarded her as she checked the computer for new online and call-in orders. "Do you like doing this?"

She shrugged. "I guess it's kinda fun. Like building little model kits you can eat."

Julius snorted a little laugh, but it faded quickly. "You know, April always loved your spinach pies."

"Yeah." Amalthea didn't look up from her work.

"Come on, Amalthea." Julius leaned over the counter again, careful to avoid the stacked boxes. "I know you care about the truth. The cops are giving up. These ridiculous monster rumors are taking over the town. Please, you gotta help me find out what really happened!"

Amalthea's shoulders tensed, her fingers tightening against the flour-sprinkled counter.

Julius deflated and stepped back, shuffling stoop-shouldered toward the door.

"When?"

Julius's expression lit up like a lighthouse beacon. "When are you done here?"

"Not until three."

"Okay, I'll come back then. Amalthea?"

She looked up at him, and he smiled, raising his hand to the door handle as her father came in from the back room, bundled up in his coat, hat, and gloves.

"Thank you."

***

"There's nothing here but police tape and a million, billion footprints."

"It's that stupid cryptid video." Julius kicked at the few clattering shells still left on the frosty beach. "Everyone and their great-aunt

Gertie have been out here looking for the monster. Look at this – this beach used to be *covered* with shells and stones. Now…"

"Practically picked clean." Amalthea stared bleakly along the sandy shoreline. "Guess they wanted souvenirs."

"So dumb." Julius squeezed his fists tight. "They'll flood out here searching for a sea monster. But my sister…"

Amalthea climbed up a muddy slope studded with exposed tree roots. "There's a bench up here," she called back to Julius. "You might want to see this."

Julius roughly wiped his eyes and climbed up after her. "What? Flowers? Teddy bears?" He frowned at a soggy little plushie with oversized glitter-eyes. "Unicorns?"

Amalthea took a few photos of the colorfully cluttered bench. In front of the toys, flowers, and little bags of candy, a semi-circle of sooty, rain-flooded candles had been arranged in the sand, held in place with piles of shells. She pulled a damp card from one of the shell piles and held it out to him. "It's a memorial. For April."

Julius dropped the card and backed away. "This is – no! She's not dead! Why would people do this?"

A twig snapped, and they turned to see a pair of police officers approaching. "Hey! I thought we told you kids to go home!"

"We're looking for my sister," Julius said angrily. "Like you should be doing! Not giving up and letting people…" He choked and swallowed, sniffing in a shaky breath. "She's not dead, okay? She's here, somewhere, and we have to find her!"

The officers shared a look. The taller one sighed and stepped closer while her partner headed for the beach. "The search isn't over," she told them. "That's why we're trying to keep this beach clear."

The sound of a motorboat revving up made Julius's expression harden. "You're not gonna find her in the water. Why aren't you searching the forest!"

"I promise, we're doing everything we can to find the missing girl."

"April," Amalthea said.

"April." The officer nodded. "Now, I'm sure you kids know there's an emergency curfew in place for everyone under eighteen. Head for the parking lot now, and you should be able to make it home before sunset."

Amalthea's lips tightened, but she turned on her heel and headed up the muddy trail. Julius glared a moment longer, then followed her.

"Amalthea—"

"We're coming back," she said. "Tonight."

"Why? Did you see something?"

"I thought…" Amalthea paused and looked back, peering into the shadows under the bare-branched trees. "I found that shrine because I saw this weird shimmer. And something else, like an electric flash. Those cops showed up before I could check it out, but—"

"I saw that too!" Julius exclaimed. "Just before April vanished, there was this bright flash of light. I thought, maybe the sun hit some sea glass or, I don't know. But if you saw it too—!"

"Tonight," Amalthea said again, and led the way back to the car.

***

Julius met Amalthea at the edge of his driveway, gesturing for her to park by the neighbor's curb.

"Sorry," he said as she got out, "but we have to be quiet. My parents think I'm in my room."

"I had to sneak out too," Amalthea admitted. "Where are we going?"

"This way. There's a path." He led her across his sloping backyard into the woods beyond. "Watch out for brambles."

Bright moonlight made flashlights unnecessary and, before long, Amalthea heard the lapping sound of waves against a muddy bank.

"Over here," Julius urged. "Josh said we could borrow his dad's boat."

"His…" Amalthea blinked, her feet firmly rooting on the sandy path. Julius hopped into the small motorboat tied at the far end of the reeds and reached a hand out to her.

Amalthea shook her head, cold reluctance freezing her from the inside out. "You didn't say anything about a boat."

"Those cops gave me the idea. We can get to Rome Point faster this way, and we won't have to walk those creepy trails in the dark. Come on, get in!"

She stared at his hand, trying to will herself to take it, to just grab his palm and step into the boat. There was no wind; the water reflected the moon and stars like a gently rippling mirror.

So, why did her heart feel like a wild bird in her chest - flapping and screaming and struggling to escape!

Amalthea's world gave a sickening lurch. Her breath quickened and she had to turn away, to walk, run faster – faster – hot, humiliated tears streaming down her face.

"Huh? Amalthea!" Julius called after her, his voice strangled with surprise.

Amalthea's shoes slapped against the uneven dirt path. This was unfair. She wanted to go back, to help—

But there was no way she was getting in that boat.

"Where are you going!" Julius's baffled shouts echoed over the water. "Amalthea? Amalthea Jones!"

***

"Look, I said I'm sorry. I didn't know." Julius stood on tiptoe, leaning even farther over the counter than usual. Amalthea refused to look at him, slapping angry sauce on two angry pizzas. "But seriously, what are you afraid of? Was it the boat? Being out on the water?"

Amalthea clenched her teeth, then threw a double-mass of cheese shreds, pepper strips, and sausage chunks down on the sauce and shoved the angry pizzas in the oven.

"Amalthea, come on," Julius urged. "How are we supposed to find April if you won't talk to me!"

The pizzeria's doorbell jangled. Julius grunted and slid back to his feet.

"Hey, Julius. We're here." April's friend Olivia waved, holding the door as more of April's school friends and fencing teammates poured into the narrow space. "You texted you want to talk?"

Amalthea kept working. Julius sighed through his nose.

"Yeah," he said. "Thanks. How about we sit down?"

Amalthea sighed, and shoved an angry meatball calzone in with the angry pizzas. The anger wasn't for Julius, though. Not really.

Truth was, she was angry at herself. Amalthea liked to feel in control. To have everything around her organized. Every puzzle solved. Every piece in its place.

Out on the bay, though, anything could happen. A stray wave, a sudden wind, a false step, and she could be knocked in the water, arms and feet flailing with no purchase, nothing solid to grab on to!

She felt the same way about lakes, ponds, public pools, anything where her toes couldn't touch the bottom. Just one of the reasons she'd never learned how to swim.

Amalthea leaned hard against the counter, fighting to slow her panicked breathing. Out in the restaurant part of the pizzeria, she heard April's friends talking, sharing stories with Julius, and tried to concentrate her mind on that.

"She doesn't suck at Morse Code," Julius was saying. "She just thinks it's boring."

"More like pointless." Annie smirked. "Anyway, April could only ever remember the numbers."

"Yeah, but she did get that trailblazing badge," Olivia broke in. "Remember, at Camp Kaufman? Ms. Jasper got totally turned around on that nature hike, so April led her whole troop back to the cabin – without a map!"

"That's why I can't believe she got lost!" Julius said. "Not in those woods, and not with the bay *right there*. I mean, you hit the beach, you know where you are. Yeah?"

"Plus, Jamestown Bridge is right near Rome Point," Marissa agreed. "The cars up there can get pretty loud. Especially over the water. She couldn't miss a landmark like that."

"Maybe the Shellycoat did take her," Alexis mumbled.

"Enough with the Shellycoat!" Julius shoved himself against the back of the booth and pulled a small silvery disk from his jacket pocket, like a large watch battery. "There's no such thing."

Olivia peered over the table. "What is that?"

"Just a holo-emitter," he muttered. "It bends light. Before all this…" He sighed. "I've been messing with a design for a holographic UV shield. You know, for cars and things. Exposure to ultraviolet light breaks down the chemical bonds in the paint and stuff. So, with my shield, you just push a button and *poof!* The UV rays are blocked before they can cause any damage. Got me to the State Science Fair. I was hoping, if I placed at State, or even won, I could snag a scholarship for physics or engineering or something. 'Cause, you know, April's gotta go to college after me, and…"

"What?" Olivia prompted gently.

Julius shook his head and stuffed the little disk back in his pocket. "Doesn't matter. I think we've been sitting here a while. Do any of you want a pizza or whatever? I'm buying."

The chatter rose and Amalthea turned back to her work, slicing and stacking orders for delivery. As she did, she cast her mind back to the day April May disappeared. She remembered the way April smiled when she and her brother walked into the pizzeria, soaking in the scents of savory toppings and yeasty dough. The way she'd bounced on her heels, pushing Julius away from the counter window so she could watch Amalthea prepare their spinach pies.

Julius. He'd been leaning over the counter, like always, talking and playing with something in his hand. She'd thought it was a coin. Bigger than a quarter, like a half or silver dollar.

But, what if…?

"Julius!"

The chatter paused, and Julius got to his feet. "Yeah, Amalthea?"

"Forget the pizzas," she said, unknotting her apron and pressing the doorbell button to get her parents down to the shop. "I know what happened to April!"

***

The late February sun had already started to sink by the time the teens made it to the beach at Rome Point. The little shrine of flowers, toys, and cards had outgrown the bench, but Julius charged right past it, down to the rocky beach.

"So, what's the plan?" Olivia asked, a little breathless from trying to keep up with Julius's long, swift strides.

"Look for a light," Amalthea told the group. "Like a shimmer, or a bright flash."

"What about this police tape?" Alexis picked nervously at the yellow plastic. "I don't think we're supposed to be here."

Olivia ducked under the tape with purpose and gestured for the others to follow. "Come on. Let's spread out and search."

While April's friends and teammates scoured the barren shoreline, shouting her name, Amalthea headed back to the shrine in the clearing. Among the flowers and shell piles, she spied a few silvery candy wrappers, and even a couple of small take-out boxes from her family's pizzeria: Anchovy's Pizza Palace.

"That's a relief."

"What, the litter?" Julius stalked irritably past her and kicked at a box.

"It means she's been eating," Amalthea told him. "At least, I hope it does. If I'm right, then wherever April is now, she's likely to come back to this place. Especially if she hears the others shouting."

Julius furrowed his brow. "Amalthea. Back at Anchovy's, you said you knew what happened to my sister. Can't you just tell me?"

"Julius!" Amalthea pointed. In the shadows, among the tangled bracken, something shimmered...then flashed!

"It's that light!" Julius gasped. "Look! It's flashing again!"

"I thought so. Do you have a pen?"

Julius patted his pockets. "Here's a pencil. Is that—"

Amalthea snatched the pencil and grabbed a pizza box from the sandy mud. "Shh! Just watch!"

The light kept flashing – long bursts and short bursts. Amalthea seemed excited, scribbling on the white inside of the pizza box, but for a long time, Julius couldn't make much of it. He could see no pattern to the flashes, no rhythm. Until…

"Got it!" Amalthea exclaimed. "I did it, Julius! I cracked the puzzle! We found her!"

"What are you talking about?"

She thrust the pizza box into his arms, pointing at her pale scribbles with the pencil. "It's Morse Code. Just like you were all talking about at the pizzeria! See? Four dots and a long dash: that's four. Five long dashes: that's zero. One dot and four long dashes: that's one."

"Four – zero – one," Julius repeated. "Okay. What's the rest of this?"

"The next group of flashes spelled out: Five – zero – one." Amalthea gestured to more scribbles.

"401, 501." Julius frowned. "Are those supposed to be area codes?"

Amalthea laughed. "Ha – that's good! I didn't think of that. Yeah, Rhode Island has a 401 area code. But, no, I think the answer's simpler than that."

"Simpler?" Julius squinted, reaching into his pocket and twirling one of his spare holo-emitters between his fingers.

"I think they're dates," Amalthea spelled out. "4-01. That's April First."

"April Fool's Day?"

Amalthea snickered. "Come on, Julius – think! 4-01 is the first day of April. So, 5-01 is the first day of?"

"May," Julius realized, his eyes going wide. "April May!"

"Annie said April never learned the letters in Morse Code."

"Just the numbers," Julius breathed. "Then, you think—?"

"Julius! Amalthea!" Olivia pounded into the clearing, flanked closely by the rest of the group – and three very irritated cops.

"I told you! I told you!" Alexis was whining. "I said we shouldn't go on that beach! Now it's past curfew, and we're gonna be arrested, and they'll make my grandma drive all the way to the police station, and we'll all have criminal records, and—"

"Shut up!" Olivia snapped. "Since when is it against the law to search for our friend? These cops—"

"Stop, everyone! Listen!" Amalthea held up her arms until the noise died down. "We found April. I'm not even kidding! She was right here – until you all came barging in…"

"What?" the gathered teens exclaimed. "What happened! Where is she?!"

"I was just about to explain!" Amalthea stepped past Julius to stand before the cluttered bench. "This has all been a terrible accident. And it's partly my fault."

"Your fault?" Julius frowned at her. "How could this possibly—"

"It's partly your fault, too," Amalthea told him. "Think back to the day April disappeared. You both ordered spinach pies, yeah? And what were you doing while I put them together?"

"I don't know. Watching, I guess."

"You were hanging over the counter," Amalthea told him. "Like I always tell you not to do. And what did you have in your hand? Do you remember?"

Julius shrugged, pulling his hand from his pocket. "I don't know. I—"

"Was it something like that?" Amalthea fixed her gaze on the silver disk in his palm.

Julius looked down at the little holo-emitter and gasped, clenching his fist tight.

"Here's what I think happened," Amalthea said, directing her words to the whole group, but mostly to the frowning cops. "You were leaning over the counter, playing with one of your holo-emitters. When April shoved you aside, I think you dropped the holo-emitter into the filling of one of the spinach pies I was making. I promise I didn't notice, or I never would have put it in the oven! I don't know if the heat damaged it or the spinach protected it or what. But it's my guess April *ate* that spinach pie, and *swallowed* your little holo-emitter. *That's* why she seemed to disappear!"

"What are you saying, kid," one of the cops said. "The missing girl isn't really missing – she got cloaked by a hologram?"

The other cops snickered. "An invisible kid?" they scoffed. "Hey, maybe *she's* the Shellycoat!"

Julius gave a start, looking positively enlightened. "Maybe she's the... And if the emitter got warped... Good grief! That's it!"

He dug deep into another pocket, pulling out a little black device, like a car key remote.

"Look, this is the remote I modified for my science fair project. If I turn the holo-emitter off..."

He took a breath and held it, then firmly pressed the button.

***

"And there she was! All sandy and exhausted." Olivia spoke over the lively crowd squashed inside the narrow pizzeria. At one table, the cops from the beach raised their pizza slices in celebration while April laughed with Julius and her friends at another. Behind the counter, Amalthea watched it all, sliding happy pizzas and calzones in and out of the oven.

"Amalthea!" April called from the restaurant, waving her arm. "Amalthea, we need you over here!"

She hesitated for a moment but, when the rest of the group took up the call, Amalthea left the counter and stepped over to April's table.

"Here, grab a slice! It's pepperoni!" Julius handed her a loaded paper plate, grinning broadly when she took it.

"Okay, everyone," Olivia called out, and raised her own slice high. "This one's for Julius May! For never giving up! Hooray!"

The gathered group took up the cheer, then everyone took a big bite.

"Here's one for April!" Julius shouted, and they all took another bite, laughing and whistling. Amalthea smiled and started to head back, but April held up her slice.

"And this one's for Amalthea Jones! Seriously, Cap – you're my hero. And not just because you saved my life out there. Here's to the best spinach pies in the universe!"

Amalthea snorted a little laugh. "You mean, you still want to eat my spinach pies, even after—"

But no one heard her bashful tease. The whole crowd had erupted in cheers – boisterous, heartfelt cheers – and Amalthea stepped back in wonder.

This feeling, it was something new. For the first time, she felt... She was *part* of something. Part of the group, the cheers, the laughter, the good smells of baking pizzas, and she had to admit...

It was something extraordinary.

Marie Ventura (Pen Name: Rowena Zahnrei), is a neurodiverse (ASD) author. She's been published in children's magazines, comics anthologies, peer-reviewed academic journals, and book format – including her graphic novel trilogy: *The Adventures of Nicki and Ricky: Baffling Birds!* Her love of folklore feeds her passion for weaving original tales.

Garnet Heart

— AA DaSilva

Don't tell me of your things
I want to know your soul

Where do you find magic?
Have you seen a ghost?

Let's talk of death and birth and finding life between the two
Let the galaxies in my eyes collide with you

Tell me of love and betrayal and grief
Tell me what you dream of when you sleep

Show me all the parts you had to chip and break and mold
To meet the standards they uphold

Gather all the broken pieces
Shattered from the parts they shunned
Now hold it up like sand glittering in the sun

Show me your pretty little garnet heart

And all the things that made them laugh or chide or step back
Show me what's behind that mask

The parts of you most precious they stole
So don't smile and speak of small things
I want to know your soul

What once made you small and outcast
Is now your power
Bring it forward in this dark hour

For those who held you down to get ahead
Knew all along the extraordinary power you possessed.

AA DaSilva believes the art of storytelling has the power to connect us on a deeper level, and that empathy is the heart of the human condition. Check out aadasilva.com to learn about her award-winning speculative romance novels, forthcoming projects, and which book events you can find her at next!

Market House

— Alfred R. Crudale

The rising sun slowly illuminated the dark waters of the Providence River. Its golden rays, creeping toward land, touching the bridges until it reached the plaza where I stand watch on the corner of College and North Main Streets. I've stood here for many years, since my construction in 1773, and I have witnessed numerous events, some mundane, others quite exciting.

In March of 1775, many people gathered on my square in protest. Late in the afternoon a fire was lit, a blaze to rival those of Gehenna, to which was added a wooden barrel filled with thick black pitch. The mob jeered and cheered as several of their members added papers and broadsides, which they called the speeches of Lord North. As the orange flames crackled, and the acrid smoke fouled the air, a large group of women marched into the square. Approaching the blaze with large buckets, they hurled heaps of tea into it. The throng cheered as they railed against the British king and his taxes.

One warm September afternoon in 1897, a crowd began to gather in Market Square when a woman, dressed in a white blouse with a lace collar, a gray waistcoat, and ankle-length matching skirt entered the square. This lady, wearing round, wire-rimmed spectacles, commanded a presence as she launched into a passionate oration which engaged and motivated the crowd. As the many females in attendance began to express their enthusiasm and consent, a large contingent of Providence policemen, accompanied by the mayor, broke through the crowd, and forcefully arrested the speaker, who they called Emma Goldman. The crowd dispersed as Emma was taken to the Providence police station, where she spent the night.

My ground floor and adjacent square served as the Providence marketplace. In the mid-1800s, the Providence City Council met on my second floor, while the Freemasons occupied the third floor. I also served, for many years, as the headquarters of the Providence Board of Trade.

September 21, 1938, however, felt very different. Something was odd about the air pressure. The pressure on the red bricks of my facade was greater than the pressure on my inside walls. Unusually strong drafts coursed through my open windows with an eerie fury.

I had not experienced these harrowing signs since the Great Gale of 1815. That was really a terrible storm. As the fierce wind buffeted my walls and windows, the turbulent waters of the Providence River rose higher and higher, until my foundation was submerged. As these thoughts accosted my memory, I realized that some diabolical affair was in the making.

By mid-morning the sky took on a strange yellowish hue, with long streaks of opaque clouds expanding over the city. The wind had increased, blowing with greater force. Crossing Market Square, men held onto their soft hats so as not to have them end up in the river, while ladies held down their skirts, trying desperately to maintain their decency. Noon found a gray overcast sky and the wind was blowing in great gusts, jangling the trolly lines and rocking lamp posts and utility poles. To my south, the white-capped river churned furiously. By early afternoon, the rain began, and the people of Providence knew we were in for quite a storm, but no one expected something so extraordinary.

The gale bore down on Providence with a menacing howl which filled the city with dread. My windows bulged inward, and slates flew from the roofs of neighboring buildings. Church spires, like sentinels under fire, swayed as the wind harassed and pounded them. The roofs of the city's buildings were no match for the relentless gale. Many were torn to shreds or, like the roof to the *Providence Journal* building, were peeled from their edifices, as if they were lids removed from a tin can. The rain poured down in sheets, driven by the unyielding gusts. The water seemed to rise with each passing minute. As they shielded themselves from the infernal tempest, pedestrians were unable to walk upright. Many, hunched so far over, appeared to move on all fours. Soon, however, the sidewalks had disappeared, as the water continued to surge, trapping drivers in cars.

Terrifying cracking and crashing sounds accompanied the battering force of the wind as it toppled trees. A young couple taking refuge in their car on Benefit Street was crushed as a stately oak tree was ripped from the sidewalk and hurled on its side atop the vehicle. Many drivers abandoned their cars, which also disappeared beneath the water. Soon after being deserted, automobiles on the Weybosset Street Bridge and the Crawford Street Bridge tumbled into the river. Several employees gathered on my third floor, and watched in horror as the river inundated the parking lot of the courthouse, covering the cars parked there. As they began to short circuit, blaring car horns, coupled with the sirens of police and fire vehicles, added an eeriness to the sounds of the furious tempest.

Towards early evening there was a frightening crash and the sound of smashing glass as several of my windows burst from the tremendous force of the wind. Water and debris poured in through the gasping spaces, drenching those who had taken refuge on my third floor. One woman was knocked to the floor, her head bloodied after being hit with a brick which had flown in through a broken window facing Market Square. The incessant roar of the wind was reminiscent of a charging locomotive. High tide was due soon, and there was no sign of the storm abating. Just about this time, something strange appeared on the horizon of the river. It seemed as though the river and sky had become one, and this new creation was bearing down on the city. Several people on my third floor screamed, while others prayed out loud, as they realized a massive wall of water was about to crash down upon Providence.

As when the gate to a sluiceway is opened and the powerful water rushes in to turn the gears of a mill, so too were Market Square and the surrounding streets engulfed when the tidal wave struck with a vengeance. Buses and trolleys were swallowed up as white-capped surf rolled through Weybosset, Washington, and Fountain Streets. The entire city was flooded. One hundred-twenty mile-per-hour winds sent walls crashing down upon sunken vehicles. Boats were wrecked against the ramparts of the bridges. One, a thirty-foot pleasure boat, sank to the bottom of the river after smashing into the rails of the Crawford Street Bridge. In 1815, the flood waters rose to just over eleven feet, but this storm was much bigger and more powerful. Following the tidal wave, the waters of this storm reached over thirteen feet, dislodging many of my bricks and mortar, and submerging my first floor.

As night fell, the winds quieted, allowing rescue teams to search for survivors. Resembling Venice, Italy, rather than Providence,

Rhode Island, the blue hue of search lights reflecting off the turbulent watery streets created a ghastly scene evocative of a Lovecraft novel.

Men in rowboats valiantly set out seeking anyone who needed help, but the current was too strong. The small crafts were tossed about like twigs on the rapids of a river; their navigators were unable to maneuver them. Looking out across Market Square to the north, the people who were now trapped on my third floor watched as plush chairs with blue velvet cushions, an ornately carved mahogany settee, and red lamp shade with black lace floated out of the smashed windows and doors of the Central Hotel. The rescue effort of the police and firemen was greatly hindered as they dodged the debris, which mingled with wooden planks and broken glass floating in the floodwaters. The hotel's electric sign was now dark, and its E, H, and T swung like pendulums in the wind.

As the rescue teams struggled to take control of the desperate situation, others with nefarious intentions took advantage of the chaos. As often happens, whenever a disaster occurs, rogues come forth and capitalize on the misfortune of others. Through the swirling water, two men entered the haberdashery across Market Square. Entering through the blown-out plate glass windows, the looters made off with their arms full of men's soft hats and bowlers, as well as women's headwear, adorned with silk flowers, or brightly colored feathers. Two doors down, three other thieves looted the sporting goods store. Wading through water up to their hips, they emerged with a stash of wooden baseball bats, leather mitts, and a net sack full of inflated footballs. Emboldened by the fact that police were occupied searching for victims of the storm, these marauders plundered Providence department stores, restaurants, and any business which they could easily pillage.

As the curtain of night slowly lifted, allowing the orange aurora to spread its beam over the ravaged city, the destruction left by the storm became visible and undeniable. In the wee hours of the morning, the river and flood waters, which had receded with the ebb tide, left streets littered with broken glass, merchandise, and building debris. The crackling sound of shattered glass could be heard as police cars and fire engines passed over it. Large trees, which had been uprooted, lay blocking streets or atop houses. Parking meters, previously cemented to the sidewalks, were twisted free and lay several yards from where they had once stood. The glass skylight of the Providence Public Library had been smashed and lay in fragments on the flooded library floor. The streets, avenues, and boulevards of the city revealed the savagery of the storm. Of course, the worst of all were the victims. As firemen, assisted by the National Guard, pulled two mangled bodies from a bus which lay beneath a toppled brick wall, they were sickened by the floating bloated corpse of a man who had drowned as he desperately tried to return to the safety of his home.

The din of chainsaws, water pumps, and generators was heard in every corner of Providence, as store owners and homeowners began the slow process of repairing. Tow trucks lined up at the courthouse parking lot to remove vehicles which could not be driven. An army of glaziers fanned out across the city to replace the hundreds of windows and glass doors destroyed by the tempest. Workmen restrung electrical and trolly lines. After the initial shock had passed, the people of Providence worked together to restore the city they so loved.

The capital city of Rhode Island has greatly changed since that fateful September day. Surrounded by its universities and hospitals, Providence is a vibrant New England city. In 1954, I watched another hurricane roar up the coast and flood Providence. It was, however, much less destructive than the storm I witnessed in 1938. Although after the '54 hurricane, Providence had had enough. A group of Rhode Island's most accomplished engineers convened to design a mechanical wall spanning the Providence River to protect the city from the fury of future deluges.

In the mid-1980s, I beheld a massive public works project which redirected the Providence River and created more green space in our capital city. No longer do I serve as a market or trade building. Following the 1938 hurricane, I underwent a series of renovations. Then, in the 1940s, my stately red brick and white trim edifice with its great round clock on my western facade just under the roof's peak was given to Rhode Island School of Design. I now proudly house many classrooms for one of Rhode Island's most prestigious universities. My square too has been redesigned to encourage walkers and tourists to relax on my park benches to contemplate the historic square where fish, meat, poultry, straw, hay, and produce were once sold to the people of the city.

Attached to the exterior of my southern wall are two plaques placed at the height of the floodwaters from the Great Gale of 1815 and the Hurricane of 1938. These plaques serve our city as a memory of two tremendous tempests which ravaged our capital. As I continue to peer southwest over the Providence River, I will forever remember the 1938 Hurricane as an event that was something truly extraordinary.

The water level marker plaques can be seen on the southern facade of Market House building at the corners of College and North Main Streets in Providence.

Alfred R. Crudale is a professor of Italian at the University of Rhode Island. His children's book, *A New Home for Salvatore*, was released by Stillwater River Publications in May of 2024. His latest children's book, *Buon Natale, Salvatore*, was released in October of 2024.

Memorial Day

— Stanley Carpenter

"Damn, it's hot!"

I jammed the A/C fan control as far to the right as possible for maximum air flow. It wasn't that hot really — more frustration and disappointment. Momma said there would be days like this, but not week after week! I knew the real estate business was fraught with disappointment, but Hell's Bells, I hadn't had a closing in three months. VISA threatened to repossess my card.

"Get with the program!" I shouted at the guy ahead in the yellow Subaru, piddling along several miles below the speed limit. I took out my frustration on everybody and anybody that muggy, late May afternoon. I wasted most of the day down in Pittsboro with a "we'd like to see a few more houses" client. What does it take? Actually, I do know what it takes to get a real estate business off the ground, but this particular afternoon halfway between Chapel Hill and Pittsboro, I just felt sorry for myself and my bad luck.

Coming over a rise, I noticed an old stone chimney standing guard in a plowed field. The ruin mesmerized me. Its top half was missing, but the base remained intact. A well-defined semi-circular hearth faced the highway. It stood in the midst of the field as it had for decades, perhaps centuries. Overgrown with weeds, it seemed a lonely monument to who knows how many generations of solid farm families, now gone. I don't know why this ruin drew me in so profoundly that all my anger and frustration suddenly seemed superfluous. As the chimney passed on the right and receded in the rearview mirror, a sudden, very odd feeling came over me – almost a feeling of serenity. Somehow, I knew that someone of great significance had dwelt there in the now non-existent house. I envisioned that significant person stretched in front of that toasty fireplace on a cold, drizzly Carolina winter afternoon.

"Oh no!" I jammed the brakes as hard as I could. Too late! I had run right up the back of the Subaru. I braced for the crash. Impact! "What the...!" I was in the guy's trunk, but no bump, no screeching tires, no crunch of metal on metal. I went through the front seat — nothing, absolutely nothing happened. I passed right through the car as if it wasn't there at all.

I slowed to a creep with pale, bloodless hands tightly gripped to the steering wheel. My heart raced two, three, four times normal pace. A bead of sweat welled up my forehead and rolled down the bridge of my nose. Gingerly, I turned off the highway onto the gravel shoulder. For a full minute, I sat shaking, never taking my hands off the wheel. Slowly, my breathing returned to normal.

Just ahead to the right, a dirt road led into the field. Why I had an overwhelming need to turn into that road, I don't know. Prying my right hand off the wheel, I put the car in drive, crept up to the dirt road, and turned in. The road meandered around through a clump of trees, as usual for these old farm roads. As I came back into a clearing, I saw a small, wood-frame barn up on the left. What I saw next gave me almost as much of a shock as the phantom Subaru. Clearly, a few hundred feet ahead, lay the highway, where I had just come from, and the same, stone chimney. Only now, that chimney was firmly attached to a small, weathered, single-story frame house.

It occurred to me that, owing to the collision, I was either dead or in an unconscious dream.

I pulled up into the rain-rutted, red clay driveway. Hens and a bantam rooster scattered and clucked as I eased the car up to the house. I smelled the oily odor of fried chicken, but, no, it's part of this dream. After all, fried chicken is to the rural South what lobster is to Maine, so, naturally, I would smell it in this particular delusion. I pulled up the parking brake.

I sat for several minutes in the car. Should I go to the simple pine-frame door, behind the slightly worse for wear screen door, and present myself? Or should I wait for someone to appear? They had to have heard me driving up on this muggy, sultry afternoon. I waited. No response. I decided to give it a go. I lifted the handle, opened the door, gently put both feet on the red clay driveway, and slowly stood up, staring without a blink at the front door. Why I did that, I don't know. How could a dream, delusion, or worse, hurt me? Nonethless, I was apprehensive. As I walked towards the front porch, I felt the urge to look back at the car. My third jolt of the day made me gasp, a short, quick stab of air. I suppose I hadn't fully accepted the dream yet. Instead of a metallic blue 2023 Honda Civic, there sat a 1939 grey Ford Coupe. Stenciled on the door, in flat black paint was "US NAVY 32578." As I turned back towards the house, I realized that rather than the grey herringbone suit with red foulard tie, I now wore the service dress khaki uniform of a US Naval Officer. I glanced over at my left shoulder and counted the gold stripes on the black shoulder board. Three. A commander. That's something, anyway. I ran my fingers over the cluster of ribbons over the left breast pocket. I did not know what they signified.

I stepped up onto the worn porch stoop. Despite the obvious age of the house and the clear poverty of its occupants, the owners took great care of their property. Begonias, pansies, and other assorted flowers bloomed in the late May afternoon sun in planters, window boxes, and, in small plots around the foundation. The house's white weatherboard exterior had been recently painted, and the yard freshly mowed. I opened the screen door and knocked.

Visitors are a serious business in the rural South. Even in the 21st century, the code of hospitality, centuries old, requires that a visitor, regardless of whom, be accorded the highest state of personal attention by the host. It was with this in mind that I heard the bustle of activity and haste from behind the knotty pine door. Seconds later, a very much surprised Black woman appeared behind the opened door.

She was archetypal, fiftyish, stout, with graying hair made frizzy and unmanageable by the humidity. She appeared well-kept despite the obvious age of her cotton print, one-piece dress and white linen apron covered in delicate embroidery of various floral patterns. She wore inexpensive, but neat leather sandals. For several seconds, we stood staring at each other, both startled by the incongruous scene. Finally, she spoke, a simple "Yes, sir, can I he'p you?"

"Mrs. McArdle, I presume. (*how did I know her name?*) "I'm Commander Gregory Wilhite, US Navy, from Norfolk."

"Oh, yes sir. Please come in. Thomas! Thomas! They's company!" She moved aside and motioned me into the parlor.

"Mr. McArdle." I nodded politely to the Black man who appeared in the archway leading into a hallway beyond, as I reached up to the brim of my khaki service hat with the gold "scrambled eggs" on the visor.

"Yes, sir, how you be today?" he responded tentatively.

There was, in the small, but comfortable and neat parlor, a peculiar tension. Every Southerner of a certain age who grew up in the segregation era, White or Black, has felt it at some time. Perhaps not so much with the younger 21st-century generations and millennials, but certainly those somewhat older. For their part, in decades past, Blacks in the South played the role of deference. The couple certainly seemed to do just that towards this uniformed White man of obvious authority (but always a wary and never quite trusting sort of attention). Those of the pre-Civil Rights era were always on the losing end of any argument, so the White man must not be angered. Privately, they may hate me, but publicly, all was courtesy and overt politeness to the White man standing in their parlor with the silent understanding of who was in charge, even in their own home.

For my part in this elaborate masque, I acted in the role of benevolent paternalism, a long-established form of race relations in the rural South. It gave the White man a sense of responsibility for his Black neighbors, whether as slaves or as tenants. It also gave him superiority. Racial hatred may bubble under the surface, but as long as the roles were properly played, Black and White co-existed. In the South, Blacks have always been hated as a race but loved as individuals. Deference to the White man allowed a Black man to be accepted, and, once the racial barrier was bridged, then the human bonding began. And thus, the South existed for centuries. And thus, we each played our respective roles in this elaborate pageant (delusion?) of mine.

"Please, sit down, sir. Elsie, get the gentleman some iced tea," he said as he simultaneously motioned towards a wing chair with one hand, and the kitchen with the other. Before I could open my mouth to decline, Elsie McArdle bustled off to the kitchen. *Why fight it? Play the part. It's a delusion after all.*

"Thank you, sir," I replied as I eased into the overstuffed chair, obviously his favorite judging from the great fanfare. A look of profound shock broke over McArdle's face. I started, suddenly very anx-

174

ious. What had I said? What had I done? As the incredulous expression on his face gradually dissolved, I realized the impact of my addressing him as "sir." I saw over his shoulder a wall calendar, graciously given out for free by the local funeral home. May 21, 1944. I pretended not to notice his shocked reaction.

Mrs. McArdle hurried from the kitchen carrying a cut glass (no doubt her finest) pitcher of tea, although there wasn't much ice to be seen. We began the usual small talk, the weather and so forth. And then I realized why I was there. It occurred somewhere between the second and third sip of the syrupy sweet, lukewarm tea.

"Mr. and Mrs. McArdle, I was your son's commanding officer."

William Tecumseh McArdle, known as W.T. to his shipmates, Petty Officer Third Class, USNR, wardroom mess steward onboard the USS *Daniels* (DD-627). "Coloreds" could serve only as mess stewards onboard Navy ships in 1944, but at General Quarters, his battle station was a 20-millimeter anti-aircraft gun forward of the bridge. That was why I sat there in the overstuffed wing chair.

"I realize that you have already received formal notice of your son's death, but…"

Before I could finish, Mr. McArdle rose, strode swiftly to an end table, and grasped the pale yellow, framed telegram, the standard Navy Department notice, sent by Western Union. "We regret to inform you, etc." The beginnings of tears welled up in Mrs. McArdle's eyes as her husband eased the framed telegram toward me. His hand, calloused by years of hard, manual labor, trembled. "Yes, sir. We got this here a few weeks back. W.T., he was our only child and…"

He couldn't finish his sentence. He choked on the image of his only child in a watery North Atlantic grave. After a few moments, Mrs. McArdle regained enough composure to speak.

"He didn't have to go into service, you know. Him bein' an only child. The Navy recruiter man down to Durham said he shouldn't go in. But our William, he was determined. You see, sir, his daddy here and his uncle Fred both were Navy men in the last war, and, Lordy, William couldn't stand the notion of not servin'- not after the wickedness at Pearl Harbor. His cousin Jimmy took him down to Fayetteville and swore he was his older brother. That was two years and three months back."

I noticed McArdle staring, not at me or his wife, but at the gold-framed, black-and-white photograph of a young, very proud, man in Service Dress Blues (crackerjacks, they're called) with the Stars and Stripes in the background.

"Your son was a special hero. That's why I've come here today."

I paused. I knew the entire story, but somehow, I needed a moment to collect my thoughts. Two small boxes bulged in my jacket side pocket. "I wanted to personally tell you about your son."

For the next twenty minutes, I told the couple about their son, PO3 W.T. McArdle, USNR. I told them about the convoy of merchant ships from Iceland to Murmansk in Russia, that especially dreadful convoy. I told them about how the *Luftwaffe* Condor bombers came out of Spitzbergen Island to wreak their particular violence on the men and ships below. I told them about the bomb that caught us in the bow, just forward of the anchor hawse pipe that killed or wounded most of the men up forward. I told them how their son, although badly wounded himself, helped to carry his dead and dying shipmates aft. And I told them how he refused to go to sick bay and went back forward to man his gun, and how he shot down a German bomber which had us dead in its sights. And finally, I told them how he died, slumped over the gunsight of the 20 MM where we found him after the attack. And when I finished telling them of the events of that frigid day in February 1944 off the north coast of Norway, I looked through the wells of tears into their sad, brown eyes. I did not see pain, or loss, or bereavement. Rather, I saw pride and joy and parent's love. I knew they would be fine. Their son, their only child, died, not as a poor, second class, "colored" man, but as a man, an American, a hero giving his last breath of life for his ship, his shipmates, and his country. They were reconciled.

I reached into my pocket and pulled out the two, rectangular boxes. I opened both and handed one each to the parents: a Navy Cross to the father and a Purple Heart to the mother. Oh, the sublime nature of these bits of metal, enamel, and ribbon. A nation honors its dead hero. The dignity of W.T. McArdle was captured in these two small trinkets. They could never replace the son, but, to the parents, they would always be there as a reminder of what he was. I thought as I sat there, silent, watching them lift the medals out of the boxes and place them side by side, two hands together, that even as horrible as war is, the human spirit of courage, integrity, and sacrifice still prevail over it all. That was the essence of these two medals, and that was the essence of William Tecumseh McArdle.

"As his commanding officer, I wanted to personally bring these to you, and to tell you the whole story of what happened that day."

I really couldn't think of much more to say, or do, and without fanfare, I excused myself with handshakes and the usual expression of anything I can do and so forth.

I stood on the porch, pausing a few moments to gaze at the sky with the late afternoon sun still defiantly scorching the earth, though just barely above the tall pines to the west. As I walked to the car, I felt profound shame and embarrassment. This young man gave his life for a country and a society that barely, begrudgingly accorded him underclass citizenship. Oh, yes, things gradually and dramatically changed, but in 1944… And yet, he did not hesitate to go far beyond what one might reasonably be expected to do. The man had a profound nobility that transcended human hatred and jealousy. Given this, what possible right did I have to complain about my life? So what if sales were down, a temporary condition. My own pettiness struck me in the face like the hot, sticky, early evening air.

As I turned the key in the ignition, the Ford Coupe became again my Honda Civic. I wove my way back along the bumpy, wagon-rutted road to the main highway without a glance back. And there, a few yards up ahead piddled the yellow Subaru. I looked over to the left, knowing what I would see. In a plowed field, stood an old stone chimney with the top half missing and the bottom overgrown with weeds. As it disappeared behind me, I smiled. Indeed, someone of great significance had lived there and tomorrow, well tomorrow, would be a wonderful new day.

This story is dedicated to: Commander Chuck Cole, USN; Commander Theodora Fields, USN; Lieutenant Commander Tony Gearo, USN; Captain Lloyd Williams, USMC; Boiler Technician Senior Chief Charlie Jones, USN; Signalman Chief Eddie Zellers, USN; Rear Admiral Julius Caesar, USN; and, General Colin Powell, USA.

Stanley Carpenter is Professor Emeritus from the U.S. Naval War College in Newport. He served for thirty years in the US Navy, retiring as a captain with multiple command and senior staff tours. He writes history non-fiction focusing on the American Revolution era and 20th-century world wars as well as action–adventure historical fiction and short stories.

Эдын (Édyn)

— M.Z. Medenciy

Present

The M1-8 helicopter blades thrummed, its roar muffled by Estrella's headset. The sprawling Siberian landscape stretched below. June weather made this all possible. "We're nearing Pristan," the guide's voice crackled through the comms. The group of cramped scientists nodded. "Pristan," the guide continued, "is the name of the hut Leonid Kulik built in 1929 to study the Tunguska event and its ramifications on the people of the area."

A faint smile touched Estrella's lips. The epicenter, which is found deep in the Siberian wilderness, is a remote location that is only accessible on foot. The event happened in 1908, and it wasn't until 1927 that enough resources were obtained to venture there. Now, nearly a century later, on the cusp of its anniversary, she was finally here. The helicopter settled, and the sounds of the wilderness replaced the fading whir of the rotors. Estrella, ignoring her team, tossed her headset onto the seat and stepped out. She grabbed her backpack from the waiting pile of gear that had arrived on an earlier trip. She followed a guide toward a secluded forest-dwelling, one of the several shelters she would utilize during this scientific expedition. As she reached for the door, a voice broke through the silence.

"Édyn?"

Instinctively, Estrella's hand flew to her starlight-colored hair, which she kept controlled under a cap embroidered with a d20 dice on it. She was used to fibbing about her locks and often told people she paid a premium to produce the final product. In truth, the radiant argent color was impossible to replicate; its tendency to flow unbridled was a different issue on its own. Satisfied her tresses were under control, she turned. A wiry Evenki woman, perhaps in her forties, stood there, a single luminous silver streak reminiscent of a falling star wove through her dark hair. Estrella's backpack hit the forest floor with a muted thud as she approached, grasping the woman's arm. A shimmering sphere bloomed around them, freezing time.

"Fear not, friend," Estrella's voice resonated directly within the woman's mind. "I see you knew my mother."

1908

"Édyn." The name materialized as visible puffs of condensation in the frigid Siberian air. So quiet and yet it found her as she drifted into the village, covered in borrowed furs beside Sayan. His hand, a steady presence, grounded her when all she longed to do was flee, to soar back to the stars and the nebulae from which she'd come. This terra, this Earth, pulsed with an unease that chilled her to her core. The land was angry and betrayed. Was she feeling the echoes of her ancestor? A celestial being, one of her kind, had descended here long ago. The Heavenly Maiden, the humans called her, arrived with her six-legged steed. She surmised that the descendants of that creature were what these villagers called "*opo*" - reindeer, though here they bore only four legs. Why had her ancestor lingered in this troubled world? It was forbidden, of course. Interacting with primitive life was a transgression against Celestial Law.

And now, months after her arrival, Édyn stood alone in a vast, formidable forest, awaiting her fate. Punishment. Hers alone. Not theirs, not the innocent lives she inadvertently endangered. She stood resolute, prepared. The Celestial Leaders could strip her of everything tangible, every material possession. But under no circumstance could they seize what the Evenki gifted her. Knowledge she never imagined caring to acquire. The delicate art of stitching, the rhythm of harvesting, and most profoundly, an understanding of principles foreign to her world of cold logic and universal law. Kindness. Forgiveness. Compassion. These were hers now, eternal, and forever etched into her being.

According to human time, it was mid-February when Édyn landed near the Evenki chums, their winter hunting huts. Exhausted from her journey, she had collapsed. Grateful for the solid ground and the cooling of the snow, she consciously decided to lie there and pondered about her choice to descend to Earth. She convinced herself the undertaking stemmed from the need for knowledge. She would collect enough information to satiate her curiosity. Édyn would then return to the cosmos without the Leaders knowing she had even left. Her plan was immaculate. She was lost in thought when she heard the distinct sound of crunching snow, followed by a loud exhale. Rolling onto her side, she found herself face-to-face with a reindeer. The creature nudged her, insistent until she stood. Placing a hand on its shoulder, she allowed it to guide her toward the chums. As she approached, she heard the name "Sayan" called out and found herself being observed by two men and two women cloaked in reindeer pelts. Their eyes held curiosity, which was unlike her kind, who regularly viewed strangers with scrutiny. Then, a man taller and younger than the others stepped from a chum, his gaze fixed on Édyn. He quickly removed his furs, draped them over her, and led her inside. It was there, within the warmth of the hut, as Sayan sat her down and offered her a hot drink, that she first heard the whisper of the name "Édyn" repeated outside the chum. Sayan placed a thick fur blanket over her legs and feet, never speaking a word, perceptive of an existing language barrier. The Evenki's immediate care struck her. No questions, no hesitation. These humans simply tended to her needs. She could have been a Celestial Leader, come to lay waste to their land, but it didn't matter. They saw a being in need and offered aid. Strange creatures. After sensing the land's anger, this unexpected kindness clearly contrasted with her expectations. Later, she would learn that "Édyn," the name given to her by the villagers, meant "wind," a tribute to how her starlight-colored hair flowed as if caught in an unseen breeze.

Sayan escorted her alone; the other hunters remained up north. The journey took two days, and she suspected he rested primarily for her sake. A smaller chum was set up between the hunters' winter chums in the north and the village to the south. She never felt fatigued or cold, yet he tended to her with unwavering attentiveness, ensuring she was always covered, his gentle eyes filled with curiosity and worry. The village was small, but the abundance of reindeer astonished her. The symbiotic relationship between the villagers and the reindeer was unlike anything she had ever witnessed. One could not survive without the other, and it was a harsh reminder of the fragility of life in this remote land.

She experienced that fragility firsthand weeks later when she saved a child who had accidentally fallen underfoot of the reindeer they were riding. Stripping off her mittens and furs, revealing the iridescent slender black gown she had arrived in, she held the child close and chanted, channeling her powers to fuse with that of the betrayed land. Using all the energy she could call upon and even pulling some unwillingly from the land, the child healed. As the child's wounds closed, she noticed the stark difference in their skin tones: the child's warm Evenki hues contrasted with her own bluish complexion. This explained Sayan's constant concern and the blankets he offered; he likely mistook her for being hypothermic. This made her laugh softly to herself. The child, now healed, crawled out of her arms and bounded to their mother. If she hadn't been here, the child would have surely passed. There were no healers nearby, well, at least none who could have handled the severity of the situation. Édyn thought she could be content to remain there, helping and contributing as their healer. She shook herself. Where did that invasive thought come from? She took a deep breath and stood up. Édyn could sense how grateful the villagers were, save for Sayan. The way he looked at her was strange. Was it upon seeing her skin exposed? Was he disgusted by her? His gaze held a silent torment. He hesitantly turned and walked away. The villagers, despite witnessing her otherworldly abilities and her obvious physical differences, continued to care for her.

Days passed, and Sayan kept to himself more than usual. Édyn discovered a new uncomfortable sensation emanating from her chest, negatively affecting her normal breathing patterns. While learning to stitch a khelmi with several Evenki women, she learned the reason for Sayan's strange behavior. Through hand gestures and visual explanations, she discovered he had lost his mate years ago during an encounter with a hungry wolf pack, which led to a reindeer stampede. If Édyn had arrived earlier, she could have saved her. The realization affected her deeply. This was immediately followed by the clarity that the "uncomfortable sensation" was sadness. Now, it had increased exponentially as she felt sadness for another's pain. She left the hut, instinctively seeking Sayan. She found him returning from a hunt, and without understanding why, she embraced him. She saw the villagers do this to one another when arriving and departing and during unspecified moments. She never truly comprehended its use.

Until now.

As his warmth enveloped her, their energies intertwined, hers flowing into his, soothing his deep-seated sorrow. She understood the purpose of these embraces. This was how humans healed. When she opened her eyes, she noticed a gentle, serene glow emanating from them. A testament to their connection and unique in its existence. This light, however, would ultimately become her undoing.

From that day forward, Édyn stayed with Sayan, ensuring he never felt alone. Days turned into weeks, and weeks turned into months. She embraced him upon his departures and his returns. When his clothing required repair, she'd happily weave thread and suture tears and rips. Once wolves attacked the herd, Sayan, along with others, returned injured. He raised his hands and refused her healing, pointing to the wounded. His refusal of her help was not the first or the last, but it always persisted until the others were fully healed. She learned to prepare food with items harvested and shared meals with him. His gentle soul always consumed what she crafted. He'd nod and smile even when she knew the food was cooked too long to be edible. He communicated with her through gestures and found objects, and she learned to do the same. They told tales in the moonlight by drawing in the snow. He recounted Evenki folklore; she, in turn, entrusted him with her secrets. His constant companionship, his smile, his concern, his kindness, these were the anchors that held her to this land. She felt metaphorical roots growing beneath her, binding her to the earth. Now she understood why her ancestor had lingered here millennia ago. Humans possessed an extraordinary capacity for welcome and compassion.

One star-speckled night, a powerful pull drew Édyn outside. She quietly brought her legs to herself and around her bed. She gently stepped around a sleeping Sayan and out the hut. While the villagers dreamed, she walked towards the reindeer herd. They parted, forming a circle around her, and in the center stood a translucent, six-legged reindeer. At that moment, she knew that the Celestial Leaders had found her. Her ancestor, the Heavenly Maiden, who had landed here generations ago, sent her the steed as a warning. The Celestial Leaders detected her presence when the embrace with Sayan had created a new energy. Celestials would never allow their existence to be known by "lesser creatures." Their response would be swift and merciless. Destruction to preserve their secrets. There were two options: stay on the land and accept death or flee the land and face judgment. Her kind cared only for the progression of the Celestial people, the purity of their line, and their dominance as a universal force. She bowed her head to the ancient reindeer and watched it disappear into the night. She looked up into the night sky in defiance. She would not allow them to harm this village.

Édyn waited until the thaw before preparing to leave. The villagers showed no surprise, making her wonder if other Celestials had visited and been wiser in avoiding detection.

She communicated her farewells and found that parting with Sayan was surprisingly difficult. Édyn had vowed to shield him from pain and loneliness. And now? She was the source. Yet Édyn knew that her desire to remain with Sayan could not eclipse her duty to protect them all. Delay was no longer an option. The night sky pulsed with the telltale signs that the Celestials had deployed a weapon. She needed to create distance between her and the village.

She remembered Sayan's hand on her cheek, the warmth of his touch, the desperate longing to stay. What has happened to her? So changed, so altered in such a short time. She opened her eyes, standing tall in the dense forest. Over one month had passed since her departure. She looked up at the morning sky and saw it: the weapon.

Sayan was primed, his body honed, his mind sharp. The biting cold nights had subsided. With careful watch against wolves and bears, he could tolerate the deteriorating hunting chum and rest overnight before setting out again. It was the embrace, the one that produced the light; it had irrevocably altered him. Édyn, in her unknowing innocence, might have overlooked the changes he had undergone. But he was tethered to her. He knew the instant she departed and felt the tremble of her breaking heart. He sensed her lingering presence and knew she hadn't left. Perhaps she was wrestling with the choice to return to her kind or remain with him on Earth. But when the raw, suffocating dread washed over him, he knew something was catastrophically wrong.

Now, he surged through the Tunguska Forest, following the phantom wind that tugged at the flora, a silent echo of Édyn and her ever-moving starlight hair, evidence she was present in the area. A hollow ache, the same soul-crushing emptiness he'd known, slammed into him. It wasn't his own. Whatever Édyn faced, he would not, could not, let her confront it alone.

It seemed like the forest had opened up to him, and there she was, gazing skyward, standing in the ethereal garb she'd worn the day they met. He slowed, their eyes locking. "Sayan," she breathed, her voice regal yet laced with a fear he felt as keenly as if it were his own. He ran, pulling her into an embrace. She resisted in a desperate attempt to buy him time, but he held fast. A wave of calm washed over her, and she surrendered, returning his embrace. The light surged back, this time a blinding brilliance that could eclipse the rising sun, and enveloped them in a radiant sphere.

"Édyn," he whispered, his voice rough. It was the first time he'd spoken her name. A moment she could have lived in forever, but the impending destruction…

"The weapon… I must stop it before it destroys your people."

Sayan tilted his head, a question in his eyes. "Our lips are still, yet I understand you. Do you understand me?"

"Yes," she laughed, a tear tracing her cheek. "Moments remain, and now we speak?"

"We've always spoken," he countered, his gaze unwavering.

"Tell me, Sayan, what is this feeling? Safety, peace, joy, wholeness… what word holds it?"

"You know," he whispered.

Sayan gently lifted her chin, and when their lips met, a seismic tremor rippled through the land, time itself suspended. How could this be forbidden? Was this the raw power of their joined energies? This all-consuming force, capable of creation and destruction… was this the true power of,

"Love," they breathed in unison.

They broke the kiss. "We cannot hold time," Sayan said, his voice urgent. "Whatever you face, we face it together."

"We will not survive."

"There is no life without you. I am forever altered."

"As am I."

Édyn nodded, her eyes fixed on the horizon. "We must make them believe the weapon made contact with the land. When time resumes, it will be swift. Hold me close. Fear nothing." Her black garb split, unfurling into vast, opalescent wings reminiscent of a butterfly's. Sayan clung to her as the luminous sphere dissipated, time rushing back. The weapon hurtled towards them from the southeast.

"Together," she whispered.

"Eternally," he replied.

They kissed. Calmness imbued throughout their souls; their hearts beat in tandem, and they ascended into the sky. The weapon never touched the Earth. Édyn and Sayan collided with it at an altitude of ten kilometers in a blinding flash that shattered the silence as it ignited and leveled the barren forest below.

Present

"Fear not, friend," Estrella's voice resonated in the woman's mind. "I see you knew my mother."

"Not me," the woman replied, her thoughts clear. "My grandmother knew her. Édyn saved her life in 1908."

"That explains your hair." Estrella smiled. "Your name?"

"Tymancha. My hair," she gestured to the streak of starlight-colored hair, "this mark has been inherited from my grandmother. Her entire family line, since the moment Édyn blessed her, we all bear this mark. You must tell me, Édyn, Sayan? What happened to them?"

"My parents are one with the universe, a conversation for another time. We can't hold this sphere much longer before they grow suspicious," Estrella warned, gesturing toward the heavens, knowing it would be moments before the Celestial Leaders detected the sphere.

"We?" Tymancha questioned.

"Yes, cousin. Your bloodline has been touched. You are helping me make the sphere happen."

Tymancha's eyes widened with the revelation.

"The sphere is deteriorating." Estella's voice carried urgency. "Inform your superior that I've requested you to be my personal guide. Tell him I agreed to donate handsomely to the society in return."

The two-day journey through the Tunguska wilderness became a shared pilgrimage. Estrella and Tymancha slipped away from the scientists and other guides, exchanging stories. Tymancha recounted the lore of Édyn's arrival and the mysterious disappearance of her and Sayan, which aligned with the explosion in the sky. Estrella spoke of their sacrifice and how Édyn and Sayan's energies traversed the universe. A new species and a new dawn for her people. Together, Estella and Tymancha walked to the heart of the Tunguska event.

"It's truly remarkable." Estrella stretched her vocal cords, "How, even today, these trees remain felled."

"Not as remarkable as how they protected our village." Tymancha lowered herself and touched the earth where Édyn and Sayan once stood. "While they lost many reindeer, and the shockwave scattered several roofs, goods, and possessions, no one in our village was harmed." She looked up at Estrella. "You know the research." She brushed her pants as she stood up.

With pride swelling in her chest, Estrella smiled and nodded.

"I've never seen my parents' physical form, but being here where it all began," she swallowed, holding back tears, "I can almost feel them. I can almost feel the resolve in the decision they made. The selflessness to protect those they love, those in need." She lifted her gaze and stared out past the human sky and into the vast expanse. "I strive to be like them. I strive to be something extraordinary."

For my incredible parents, Sonnia y Alvaro.

Ecuadorian-American author **M.Z. Medenciy** delights in crafting fantastical worlds. Her debut novel, *Island Eight*, won the 2023 International Latino Book Award. She is a proud member of ISLA and ARIA. M.Z. resides in the Ocean State with her husband, two sons, their pups, and one cat to rule them all.

Life is a Swing

— Debra Zannelli

It's the kind of night that contains silence
The songs of day now hushed
The breeze touches me softly
Lilac and daisy scented
In the remaining light, I feel at peace
Legs pumping, I begin to sing
Life is a swing

Impatient voices come from far away
Words galloping on the breeze
I wonder if they see
What they allow to slip away
But they rush away and lose today
They never stop to sing
Life is a swing

Days drift into years
Years simply float away
Still they do not know
Yesterday's too quickly gone
Tomorrow always a day away

Today is their one chance to sing
Or sit upon a swing

With all they miss
They just exist
So much is lost
Such a heavy cost
Life, a beautiful, remarkable thing
Is waiting for them
 to sit upon a swing.

Debra Zannelli was raised in Cumberland and now lives in Exeter. In 1996, during her recovery from surgery, she wrote *Dark Night of the Soul*. Deb has since written seven books and received honors for science fiction from Bookfest. When not writing she enjoys hiking with her dog and traveling with her husband.

Find Deb's books at

https://amazon.com/author/debrazannelli

https://books2read.com/debrazannelli

Grandmothers and Guardian Angels

— *Debbie Howarth*

Nora Hayes settled in at one of the long wooden tables, trying not to disturb the other readers and researchers at the Providence Athenaeum. The almost 200-year-old library was her home away from home, even including her on-campus office at the university. The Providence Athenaeum, particularly the alcove that housed *The Rhode Island Collection*, was her library, or at least where she went when she needed to do a deep dive into her genealogy clients' history – when online genealogy sites wouldn't do. Nora had been researching the Moores, the family of her latest client. She was reviewing the Rhode Island historical resources in the collection as she had done countless times. But this time, between *Fish of the Narragansett* and a book about Rhode Island shellfish, Nora noticed a book tucked in the back. She pulled it out, and saw *The History of Riverford, Rhode Island Community Church and Members' Recipes through the Years, 1910-1960*. Nora leaned in at the table and pored over the new-found treasure. Her grandmother Eleanor "Nellie" (McBride) Hayes had been a lifelong member and married her grandfather, Sean Hayes, in that church. Both had passed away before Nora was born, so she was always a sponge for any information about them. Nora's parents and older siblings had long since passed away as well, so there was no one to share the stories of her family history, one of the reasons Nora, a history professor, parlayed her work into family genealogy.

Nora was amazed at how active her family was in the church. Her father's baby picture was in the 1920s "Crib Roll." Her family had raised money for the upkeep of the church and its various missions – she could barely make out the images in the grainy photographs. Then she stopped when she saw them: her grandmother's recipes for shepherd's pie, Irish stew, soda bread, Ulster Fry, coddle, barmbrack, and apple cake. Nora had never seen those recipes. As she read on, she learned the book was a church fundraiser. The women of the church had shared several recipes each to be able to fill the book. Each woman was introduced and shared a bit of information about the recipes.

Mrs. Sean (Eleanor McBride) Hayes

"My family came from different parts of Ireland, and found each other once they arrived in the U.S. Our family's recipes show the variety of Irish cookery, and I am honored to share my family's recipes with you. May your grandmothers and guardian angels be watching over you, may you feel their presence in the wind, and may you think of them when you try each recipe."

Nora laughed. Glad she had added her maiden name. Grandma grew up in Riverford, and McBride was a more well-known name than Hayes in those parts. She took snapshots of her grandmother's recipes, eager to try them herself.

***

The next day, Nora was sitting in her office at the University of Narraganset Bay in Barrington, Rhode Island. She was thinking about the nightmare she'd had and wasn't getting much grading done. She went for coffee in hopes of focusing more on the task at hand. She liked the on-campus café near the Arts & Sciences building. Nora ordered her usual extra-large mocha coffee with almond milk, and found a small table near the window that looked out over the sunny quad. The spring flowers were in bloom and while still chilly, students lay out on the steps of the library, "the beach," to take advantage of the sunshine.

"Nora, mind if we sit?"

"Sure, Beth." Nora made room for Beth and her guest.

"Nora, this is my brother, Jon, he's just joined the English department."

"Jon, great to meet you. I'm in History." Nora smirked, wondering if he caught her pun.

"Aren't we all?" Jon chuckled. "Great to meet you too."

Jon Chrisman seemed more outgoing than his sister Beth, a Botany professor. Beth was quiet, but was always up for one of Nora's impromptu adventures to the beach. Misquamicut and Matunuck were their favorite Rhode Island beaches. Nothing was better than a day at the beach with a stack of reading material, then finishing with a lobster roll or fried clams. Nora always enjoyed Beth's report on the flora of Rhode Island along the way.

"What is your research area, Jon?" Nora asked.

"Early European dialects, and cultural changes through history."

"Sounds interesting. What areas are you focusing on?"

"Anglo-Saxon/Germanic."

"Jon is focused on the cultural components, folklore, customs, traditions," Beth added.

"The history of language and specific dialects makes the research into the culture so much richer," Jon said.

Nora nodded; it sounded fascinating.

Jon looked directly at Nora. "What's *your* area of research?"

"World history during the 17th-20th centuries."

Beth laughed. "Don't let Nora fool you, her real research area is family genealogy."

"Oh wait, were you the one who helped Beth last year find our dad's great-great-uncle, Henry? The one who was a captain in the War of 1812?"

"Yyyess! Nora was the one who hunted him down!"

"Thank you for finding Uncle Henry, that made Dad's year!" Jon said.

Nora nodded, then Beth squealed, "Wait until you see what we have cooked up for Dad's birthday present!"

Jon leaned forward, waiting for them to spill the beans.

"Nora completed the research on both sides of Dad's family going back to the 1400s, including documents! We had it bound with extra pages so Dad can keep adding to it – it is so beautiful – Dad's going to love it!"

"He absolutely will!" Jon agreed. "Going back to your research area, why world history from the 17th century through the 20th century?"

"There are so many young people who think history is boring until they can see how their family fits into it. There are so many tools, even just between document and newspaper search sites, where young people can learn about history in the context of their own families – we are all history. I create programs for K-12 schools to help them teach history at each grade level. The summative research shows that students are more engaged in history this way."

Beth took a long look at Nora. "Nora, you look tired, is everything okay? What are you working on now?"

"Right now I have a huge stack of papers to grade. But I'm having trouble focusing, so I was hoping the coffee would do the trick. I didn't get much sleep last night, which is compounding the problem."

"Why? What's going on?" Beth asked while Jon looked concerned.

"Stupid nightmare," Nora grimaced.

"A nightmare?" Beth and Jon said in unison.

"Yeah, it's one I've had since I was a little kid." Both Beth and Jon, surprised, motioned to Nora to share.

"It's pretty weird," Nora said. "Are you sure you want to hear this?" They both nodded their heads in anticipation.

"When I was in first grade, around age six, some of my classmates were talking

about going to church. So I went home and asked my mom about church. You never saw my mother answer yes so fast, and that we could go on Sunday. With two small children, she had stopped going, but this was her 'in' to start back up again. My dad watched my little brother so Mom and I could go. The nightmares started the Saturday night before going to church. I was in a great big church. It had four sections of pews, a balcony in the back of the sanctuary, and all of the items you would expect at the front – an altar, pulpit, organ, piano, and choir loft. A few people still remained but were about to leave after services, except my dad was sitting in the first section of pews, both in the middle of the section and the pew itself. I walked over to him, and he broke the news, telling me he had died and was waiting to go to heaven. I woke up in a cold sweat." Nora shook her head at the memory, then continued.

"I was so nervous about going to church the next day. Of course, the church we

attended didn't look anything like the one in my nightmare. Our church was smaller, had more modern woodwork, and the windows let in sunshine and a cool breeze. It was a nice place, everyone was friendly, and I enjoyed it. I've had this same nightmare over and over again, now going on fifty years. The nightmare only changed once and has stayed the same since. My older brother Sean and my sister Ellie joined my dad; they would stand behind him, and he always sat in the same pew," Nora lamented.

Beth and Jon looked at each other and back at Nora, wondering what the significance was.

"My dad was much older than me, my siblings were older too. For years, I just thought it was a weird, scary nightmare. I've never been in a church that looks like the one in the nightmare."

Beth and Jon were on the edge of their seats, feeling the anticipation of the shoe about to drop.

"Several years ago I realized that they were the first three people to pass away in my family. My dad, my brother Sean, and my sister Ellie. It's like I knew, not when, of course, but that it would happen. My mom and sister Jane passed later, but I was much older then."

"There must be a logical reason for everything," Beth rationalized.

"I've read something about these types of premonitions in my research. Let me take a look and see what I can find," Jon said.

"Thanks, Jon. It's strange that I'm still having this same nightmare. Since they've passed, you'd think that the nightmares would've stopped, or moved on to other family members? That's why I think it's weird."

***

Nora went home after finishing her grading. She wanted a week-end free of university work. Her Monday classes were already prepped, and she was looking forward to a quiet, restful weekend. She opened her refrigerator door and saw the old Chinese take-out container and her breakfast protein shakes. "Yeah," she muttered, remembering she was supposed to stop at the store before going home. She debated whether she should order out. Nora made a shopping list and, after changing her clothes, decided to go back out to the grocery store. As she began her shopping list, Nora remembered her grandmother's recipes on her phone. She pulled them up. Hmmm, shepherd's pie, Irish stew, and apple cake all sounded delish. She copied the ingredients to her shopping list on the phone, but she went back and forth about the Irish stew.

"I think I have to work up to mutton. Let's start with beef for now." Though she had shepherd's pie on her mind for dinner.

As she entered the grocery store, she heard a familiar voice.

"Wow, twice in one day, boy am I the lucky one!" Nora turned around to see Jon Chrisman grabbing a cart.

"Hi, Jon, small world; though Barrington is really a small, close-knit community."

"I'm learning that. I've visited Beth before, but it's different now that I live here. What are you buying?"

"I was doing some genealogy research up at the Providence Athenaeum, and found tucked away behind some other books, one about my grandparents' church in Riverford. There were several of my grandmother's recipes in it that I've been meaning to try. I needed groceries so I thought it might be nice to try a few this weekend."

"What are you making?"

"Shepherd's pie tonight and Irish stew on Sunday, with some apple cake I thought would be nice. Though I am starting with beef in the Irish stew instead of mutton." Nora tried to say mutton with an Irish accent.

"Yeah, I'm not a big fan of lamb, either."

"Are you free tonight? Would you be game for some shepherd's pie?"

"Sure, I'd say I'll bring the wine, but I think Guinness would be better."

"Agreed!" Nora gave Jon her address. After paying the bill, she headed home to start cooking.

***

"That was a fantastic shepherd's pie, and the green salad was delicious, too."

"The Guinness was a good call!"

"Thanks. Oh, I wanted to ask, can I see the pictures from the book?"

"Sure." Nora pulled them up on her phone. The phone started with the last one first. As Jon flipped through the phone he stopped on one photo in particular.

"Do you see something?" Nora asked.

"I was looking at the message your grandmother wrote," Jon said as he showed Nora the image.

Mrs. Sean (Eleanor McBride) Hayes
"My family came from different parts of Ireland,
and found each other once they arrived in the U.S.

Our family's recipes show the variety of Irish cookery, and I am honored to share my family's recipes with you. May your grandmothers and guardian angels be watching over you, may you feel their presence in the wind, and may you think of them when you try each recipe."

"The line, 'may your grandmothers and guardian angels be watching over you, may you feel their presence in the wind, and may you think of them when you try each recipe.' That line is really interesting, 'grandmothers and guardian angels.'"

"Yes, I liked that line too. I'm not familiar with guardian angels. Of course, I've heard of them but am not familiar."

"In some faith traditions, guardian angels are more important than others. Here, grandmothers, like guardian angels, watch over and are protectors of children," Jon explained.

"I never knew my grandmother. She passed away a few years before I was born. My dad talked about her cooking and her vegetable gardens, her civic organizations, but I don't know much else. My older brother Sean remembered being little, and often spending nights at her house and how good she was to him."

"Let me take a look at some of my books on Irish culture and traditions. See if they can shed some light. Where is your grandparents' church?"

"The Community Church in Riverford."

"Riverford, Rhode Island?"

"Yes," Nora said sheepishly.

"It's just a half hour away and you haven't been there?"

"Churches are sacred places. It feels strange going to one if you don't know anyone. It's different if it's your church or you've been invited by a friend."

"What about your genealogy research? Haven't you ever gone to a church as part of your work?"

"Of course, for a client. Going to my grandparents' church didn't have much of a draw before finding the book. There's no family still in the area to visit."

"We'll have to go, but let me do some research on that line first."

"Okay, when you say 'we'll' does that mean you'd come with me?"

"Sure, if you want me to."

"That'd be great."

After dinner, Jon headed home, and Nora checked the church's website to find out their hours and see what it looked like. The church was open daily from 9-5PM and after 5PM for church and community programs. The website was under construction, so the only picture was of the exterior of the church. Nora was surprised she couldn't find any interior pictures online.

***

A few weeks later, Nora was packing up her office in the History Department, getting ready for summer vacation, which meant her genealogy work full-time. There was a knock at the door. At the end of the school year, there seemed to be a revolving door of students in her office asking for extensions, extra credit, and mercy. With graduation just days away, the line to her office had diminished.

"Come in."

"Hi Nora, is this a good time? I'm sorry, I realize now I should have called first."

"Oh hi Jon, come in, it's a good time, what can I do for you?"

"I had an opportunity over the weekend to look into your grandmother's quote. I went through my collection of books and manuscripts on Irish culture, and a friend in Religious Studies gave me some information on guardian angels." Jon opened his notes. "In Irish culture, both grandmothers and guardian angels have similar roles, and it is thought that grandmothers are often guardian angels."

Nora was pleasantly surprised to see all of the work Jon had done.

"People view guardian angels as guides and defenders, offering hope and support during difficult times, protecting people throughout their lives," he added.

Nora looked at Jon incredulously as he continued.

"In addition, strong women are held in high regard in Irish culture— you can see it in many of their legends and folklore. These women often are grandmothers or elder women, who heroically look after young people, especially children. Grandmothers maintain the family lore, keepers of knowledge, history, and culture. Even if they haven't met, the granddaughter may feel a direct connection to her grandmother, receiving her fortitude, courage, and faith. While the explanations differ in various regions of Ireland, the belief of a powerful bond between grandmothers and granddaughters is deeply rooted in Irish culture."

"I wasn't aware of the strong connection between grandmothers and granddaughters." Nora tried hard to hold back her tears.

Jon continued, "In Irish culture, the relationship between grandmothers and granddaughters runs so deep that it is not bound by time or space. Grandmothers can offer love, protection, and guidance from another realm, even if the two never met on Earth. This connection might be through an angelic presence, food, music, images, objects, and even places the grandmother knew when she was alive.

"Oh, and here's another thing, you know how when people talk of ghosts and spirits, children are more receptive to them because they haven't been taught to not believe yet? Similarly, children may describe interactions with guardian angels as providing hope, joy, reassurance, and even strong feelings, helping them choose right from wrong. Also, it's believed that guardian angels can work through friends or strangers to support and help their charges."

The presence, Nora thought to herself, then said, "When I was a kid and would have those nightmares, or any nightmare for that matter, I'd wake up in a cold sweat, and the hairs on the back of my neck felt like it was standing up. I could've sworn there was someone in my room with me. Of course, when I turned on the light, no one was there."

"Interesting." Jon leaned back, thinking for a few moments.

"Jon, what did you say about connections to a grandmother's past life? The connections would be based on who the grandmother was, when she was alive?"

"I was thinking about the line in book you found, 'may you feel their presence in the wind.' The Irish are connected to the natural world. The wind is considered a dominant force, you see it often in their folklore and literature, especially their poetry. One of the legends describes the wind as, 'it carries the souls of ancestors, passing on information and blessings through the ages.'"

"That's so beautiful!" Nora thought for a few moments. "My grandparents spent a great deal of time at their church in Riverford. I've always wanted to see it and, I wonder, is there a connection? If there is one, I may feel it there?"

"That's possible, do you want to take a trip?"

"Yes, you'll come, right?"

"I wouldn't miss it!" Jon said enthusiastically.

***

It was a bright sunny day when Nora and Jon drove to Riverford to visit her grandparents' church. Riverford is located in the north-western part of Rhode Island, near the Connecticut border. It is a small town set in a valley with green hills around it. The Ponaganset River flows nearby and was once a source of electricity for local mills years ago. Today, the population consists of middle-class profession-als, small business owners, and those in the skilled trades. The town experienced growth in the late 19th and early 20th centuries due to the expansion of textile mills and related businesses in the region. As Nora and Jon drove through town, they saw well-kept homes and streets, and inviting businesses brimming with civic pride. The town square was the focal point with walkways that looked like the spokes of a wheel leading to a library, a diner, a hardware store, a pet store, a dentist office, and in the center, a small park with monuments re-membering the town's veterans.

The Community Church of Riverford was built during the afore-mentioned economic expansion. The church was a mix of Gothic Revival and Romanesque Revival with its stone and red brick exte-rior, conspicuous bell tower and strong buttresses used to support the large, pointed arch, framing the stained-glass window in one portion of the church, and rounded windows and doorways in the other. The church had originally been built by one denomination, but when they ran out of funds, another completed it. It offered examples of two architectural styles representing the two groups that saw to its completion. Over time that denomination left, and the Community Church members bought it.

Nora had made an appointment with the minister, the Reverend Paulson. Rev. Paulson greeted Nora and Jon as they entered the building.

"Good morning, Ms. Hayes, welcome to Riverford Community Church."

"Thank you, Reverend Paulson, it's nice to meet you. This is my friend, Jon Chrisman."

"Reverend Paulson, nice meeting you."

"You as well, Mr. Chrisman."

"Please call me Jon."

"Yes, and please call me Nora as well."

Having entered from the parking lot, they went past several offices. Reverend Paulson pointed out the Sunday school classrooms and nursery. Then they walked up a small flight of stairs that led to the sanctuary. Reverend Paulson held the door so Jon and Nora could enter before he walked through to show them the altar and pulpit area. Nora stopped dead in her tracks. Her legs felt like jelly. She was in the church from her nightmare. It was exactly as she saw it in her dreams. The four sections of pews, the balcony, and the chancel, where the altar, pulpit, organ, piano, and choir loft were; even down to the woodwork was the same. She had asked her mother years ago if she had ever been to her grandparents' church and was told no, they had never been there.

"It's the church from my nightmare, and it is exactly the same."

Jon explained to Reverend Paulson about Nora's family and the nightmares she'd had over the last fifty years. Once Nora could move her legs again, she slowly walked over to the area where her father always sat, with Sean and Ellie behind him, in her dream. She sat down, trying to steady herself to the space. She wasn't sure if it was the right pew. She then got up and moved back a pew before starting to cry. Jon and Reverend Paulson rushed over; by then, Nora was seated in the pew where Sean and Ellie always stood. Jon and Reverend Paulson stood where Nora had always stood in her dream. Nora pointed to the area to the right of the hymnals in front of her.

Jon read aloud the old brass tag on the pew in front of Nora: "Given in memory of Sean T. and Eleanor M. Hayes by their loving family – 1967."

"That was the year after Grandma died," Nora said through her tears.

Jon sat down and put his arm around Nora to comfort her. "Remember the quote from the book, 'May your grandmothers and guardian angels be watching over you...,' it looks like she has. She forewarned you of what was to come to prepare you, and even though everyone has passed away, she led you back here, so you could know that she sees you. She loves you. She is watching over you and has been your guardian angel for your whole life."

Debbie Howarth, Ed.D., a university professor, joins her interests in family genealogy-historical fiction for "Grandmothers and Guardian Angels," her second ARIA publication, which she dedicates to her Irish grandmother, Clara Lawson Howarth. Her first was "Christmas in Watch Hill" (2022). She's writing her first novel and resides in Plainville, Massachusetts.

Bourbon and Sapphire

— Roselyn Peterson

It was as if she didn't want anyone to notice her. Her head hung low, icy blonde bangs falling into her eyesight, creating a shadow across her face, as she stared into her drink. From a quick glance, she looked just *plain*. She wore a pair of blue jeans, a gray hoodie, very little makeup and almost no jewelry. Nothing extraordinary immediately stuck out. But then at a second glance, you could tell she had been crying by the slightly red color in her eyes and dark circles that framed them, and the faintest glimmer of a tear in the inner corner of her right eye. If I had to guess, I'd say she was dealing with a breakup, maybe a bad deal at work, or even the loss of a loved one. Whatever it was, it sure seemed to be bothering her to the point where she was already on her second Blantons…neat.

She has good taste in bourbon, I'll give her that. Most basic girls who look like her order a vodka soda, margarita, maybe a hard seltzer. The way she asked whether we serve Blantons before ordering it tells me she is aware it is an allocated whiskey, only sometimes offered to bars if there happens to be an extra bottle on the distribution truck. This also tells me she's been through something in her past, but what? And why is she here the day after Christmas, alone?

As someone who has been in the hospitality industry since the age of sixteen, I've seen my fair share of strange and peculiar things.

Bar fights, affairs, and as I got older, propositions for threesomes. I started working at this bar, The Bubble, about five years ago. I was sitting exactly where she is now, having just moved to this small fishing town. It was New Year's Day, 2021, and I was fighting off the meanest hangover I'd probably ever had. I had gotten into an argument with my mom the night before about not being able to find work since finishing college. I was telling my sob story to the bartender, who happened to also be the owner. He threw me a towel and told me to make a cup of coffee and get to it. The rest is history.

***

She doesn't even have her phone out, she is simply staring into her bourbon, as if it might disappear if she takes her eyes off it.

The frigid wind whipped the door of the dusty bar shut. I immediately looked over at the stranger to see if it caused her to jump, but she didn't move a muscle. Odd.

Cam clambered over to his stool where he pulled off his gloves and ordered the usual, a Miller Lite and a shot of Jameson.

"What's new, man?" I asked.

"Not a whole lot, just hiding from the family for a second while the girls go shopping, probably to return the gifts they got yesterday." He swigged his beer while surveying the interior of the dingy bar. Cam, a police officer, was married to Trina, who owned the bakery down the street. Their daughter, Kyla, worked there too. Cam and Trina were living proof of the quintessential small town high school lovebirds' story. Again, nothing extraordinary.

He nodded toward the stranger while making eye contact with me. I gave him an unknowing shrug.

***

At the end of the shift, long after Cam had arrived at The Bubble, we got stuck in our usual conversation. How was the bakery doing? How's work? How's his dad doing in the retirement home? Before I knew it, I glanced over to where the stranger had been sitting, and all that was left was a $50 bill sitting next to the empty glass. I was unsure what I did to earn a $10 tip. How strange, I thought.

"Who was that?" Cam asked, obviously intrigued by the newcomer.

"Not sure, didn't speak much," I replied.

"She sure was a looker, kind of a weird vibe though. Wonder what that was about."

"Who knows."

***

As a bartender, it's not unheard of to get home from work between 3:30 and 5:00 A.M. Tonight I am walking through my apartment door at 4:15 A.M. I had been turning it over in my palm the whole walk home. A small, delicate ring with a single sapphire in the middle. The band was silver, intricate, and complex. It glimmered in the light, lying on the floor after the last customer had left. As I was cleaning up, I put the last stool upside down on top of the bar to sweep and saw it there, right where the stranger had been sitting.

Typically, when I get home, the first thing I want to do is shower the busy shift from my body, eat something quick like a frozen waffle, and settle on the couch while listening to the morning news and drift off for a quick nap. I'm not the type of guy to sleep all day. I usually get two to three hours before getting to whatever it is that needs to be done for the day: laundry, shopping, fixing things around the apartment.

As I was listening to the morning news report on a Massachusetts man found dead at home after what appeared to be an altercation, I kept turning the ring over in my hand. "Who are you? And will I ever see you again?" Her hair as blonde as snow falling was the last thing I pictured before dozing off. Unfortunately, I wasn't scheduled to go into work until the following night, so if she went back to the bar for her ring today, I wouldn't be there. I made a plan to swing by anyway around the same time she was there yesterday in case she stops in.

***

Tony is behind the bar tonight. While Tony is a good worker, he isn't the type of guy I usually choose to hang out with and talk to. He often talks to hear his own voice and brag about his stock portfolio and bitcoin investments. I typically prefer to keep things a little less serious and stuffy.

"Hey Tony. How's it going today?"

"Elliott! Funny seeing you here on your day off. I'd have thought you'd be catching up on sleep. Started off slow here today but I'm thinking we'll get busy later, seeing as how it's Friday and all. What's new, man, how was your holiday? Santa bring you everything you asked for?"

Ugh. Tony. Small talk.

"Yeah, my holiday was great. Just thought I'd stop in for a quick drink. I'll take a Fernet please." I caught a quick glimpse of myself in the mirror behind the back bar that held our extensive liquor selection. I was particularly proud of our modifiers, Amaro Nonino being my favorite nightcap to finish off an especially long shift. My reflection reminded me of my own dark eye circles and unkempt brown mop of hair, which was telling me I needed a vacation, and soon.

"Sure thing, bud."

As he slid the shot over to me, I asked, "Hey, you haven't seen anyone new around, have you? There was a girl in here yesterday and I was wondering if she came in again today."

"Ooh, a girl? I see now. Nah, man, haven't seen anyone yet, just the usuals so far."

"Alright, thanks, man." I was hoping he'd leave it at that.

"You planning to ask her out?"

Ugh. Tony.

"Ha no, she forgot something, so I just wanted to return it to her. Totally not a big deal though."

"Alright!" He took my hint that I wanted to be left alone. "Well, I'll keep an eye out," he said as he walked over to the patrons at the other end of the bar who had been trying to flag him down.

Finally, some quiet to think. But really, there wasn't much to analyze about this girl. Blue jeans. Gray hoodie. Blonde hair. That's it really, and the ring that was burning a hole in my pocket.

The door slammed. I glanced up. It was Cam's wife, Trina. She caught my eye and sat down on the stool next to me.

"Hey, Elliott. Seen Cam yet? We're meeting here before catching a show at the community center."

"Not yet. What show?"

"Some holiday special the high school is putting on. Kyla is in it." Then she shouted, "Hey Tony! A couple Miller Lites and Jamesons, please!" Trina was your typical loud, blunt, New England woman. I always admired their gumption. "Anyway, what's new, Elliott? Have a nice holiday?"

"Yeah, not much, to be perfectly honest. Didn't really do much for the holiday."

"Eh, that sounds like it could be nice though," she said as Cam came in and took a seat at a table. Trina sauntered away, carrying the drinks over to him.

The door opened again. It was the stranger. She looked around and spotted the only open stool where Trina had just been. I glanced back toward the bar before we made eye contact, but I could feel her walking toward me. Before Tony could say anything embarrassing, she ordered a Jameson. I ordered another Fernet. *Say something to her, Elliott. Don't miss this chance.*

"Uh...hey. You were in yesterday, right? You ordered a couple Knob Creeks?"

She glanced over at me. Our eyes met. It was as if someone had just turned the lights on to the *whole world*. While her stunningly sapphire blue eyes lit up, the muscles in her face remained unchanged. The circles under her eyes seemed darker; the corners of her lips, while remarkable, remained turned slightly down. Her bangs still fell into her eyes and her hoodie was up, hiding the rest of her hair.

She just kept staring, as if she was unsure how to respond. And then, her voice, as beautiful as birds singing sad songs on a bright summer day. "Yeah, uh...Blantons," she responded cautiously.

"That's right. I thought so. I have something I think might be yours. See, I'm usually on the other side of the bar. And as I was cleaning up last night, I found this." I slid the ring over to her.

She stared at it. There was obvious recognition of the ring, but instead, she made the slightest of faces and remarked, "Uh no, that's not mine."

"Oh. Are you sure? It was on the floor right under where you were sitting and no one else sat there the rest of the night. We aren't really very busy this time of year." Why am I trying to explain the flow of the business to her right now? Am I trying to impress her with this little bar in this tiny fishing town?

"It isn't mine. Sorry," she repeated.

"Okay, no problem. Hey, I haven't seen you around here before yesterday. Are you new in town? Here for the holidays?" She seemed to be getting annoyed at this point. "I'm sorry. I mean if you don't want to talk, that's fine too. Just thought I'd try to extend a friendly olive branch. Feel free to ignore me."

Then, from across the bar, Tony yelled, "Another round, Elliott?" I gave him a thumbs up to keep him from interrupting more.

"Hey, would you like another too?" I asked the stranger.

"Sure." She was a woman of *so* many words.

"Okay, great," I said. Tony dropped off my shot and I ordered another for her as well. At this point, my best bet was to sit in silence until she said something. It felt like an eternity, but thankfully a football game was on, so I acted interested in the game.

After her new drink arrived, she murmured, "Hey, thanks. I appreciate the kindness."

"No worries. Happy to be of service," I said, secretly ecstatic she had restarted the conversation.

"I *am* new to town. Moved in just a few days ago. I just…thought it was time for a change," she offered.

"Oh, nice. Why did you choose here? If you don't mind me asking. Conanicut isn't usually a destination."

"I'm not sure, to be honest. Just seemed nice and quiet."

She was so cautious, her mind seemed to be working in overdrive, and yet her words were so few. And yet, there was something about her that was…*electrifying*. The simplicity she exuded gave off an unreal intricacy that I couldn't quite comprehend, a complexity akin to the ring I found. And those eyes were a deeper blue than the deepest of oceans, the calm just before an exceptionally stormy day.

"Well, Conanicut is definitely quiet. And we're usually nice." She didn't laugh at my subtle joke. "Hey, what's your name?"

"It's…Sofia," she said, hesitantly.

"Well, it's nice to meet you, Sofia. I'm Elliott."

"Nice to meet you too." It was as if it took all her energy to verbalize the sentence. What has her so spooked? What was the source of those dark circles under her eyes?

"So, any questions about the town I can answer for you?"

"Um, not that I can think of. I found that bakery, Kyla's, which has the most amazing chocolate croissants. And I found this bar. What else am I missing?" she inquired.

"Well, gosh, I mean, yeah, that covers the basics. There's a grocery store up by the firehouse, and a movie theater over on Main."

"You two heading over to the movies? Damn, Elliott, you move quick!" Tony interjected. "Take it from me, ma'am, this is the best guy you'll find in town. Look no further than my man Elliott."

Ugh. Tony. The man can never just keep to himself.

"Barkeep! Two more beers and shots over here," Cam exclaimed. Thank God for nice guys like Cam.

"Sorry about him," I said to Sofia. "He's kind of a know-it-all."

"Hey, no worries. You know I should probably get going anyway. I'm still setting up the apartment and stuff but…it was nice to meet you, Elliott. See you around."

"Yeah, nice to meet you…" She was already halfway to the door "…too."

***

214

Why did this keep happening? I couldn't help but feel left with more and more questions after every interaction with her. After she left, I had given up on trying to figure out who the owner of the ring was, and set it on the windowsill behind my kitchen sink, next to my favorite picture of Mom.

The next night at work Sofia came in closer to closing, around 1:00 A.M.

Cam was in and gearing up to leave when he glanced over at her. This time, he didn't stop staring at her. He waved me down.

"Man, I swear I know her from somewhere." Cam was unaware of how loud he was, and I could tell Sofia was listening. "You two spoke yesterday when you were in, right? What did you find out?"

"Not a lot, man," I said, under my breath. "She's a woman of very few words."

"Strange. Guess I'll have to do some investigating," he said, as he stood up a little too abruptly and the inertia of gravity caught him off guard for a second. "Woof - too much tonight, Elliott. Oh well, at least I'm off work tomorrow. See ya then, stay safe."

"You too. Tell the girls hi for me."

I walked over to Sofia, who seemed entranced by the liquor bottles behind me. "So, what'll it be tonight?"

"Uh, happen to have any Weller hiding back there?"

Wow, she knows her stuff.

"Not here, but it turns out I was able to find a bottle at the local package store last week, Antique 107 red label. I've been looking forward to trying it out, I've only been able to find the green and black labels before."

"Oh yeah, I have heard that's a really good one. I'm sure you'll enjoy it. My favorite is the white C.Y.P.B. one."

"Hey, what got you so interested in whiskey? Where did you get all this knowledge from?" I pried.

"Just something I enjoy, I guess. Something I've missed recently...enjoying things."

Man, was she cryptic.

"Well, you're welcome to come on over after I clean up the bar and try it out. If that's not too weird or whatever. I promise I'm not a serial killer."

"Ha. I wasn't thinking you were, well, until now." She laughed, nervously. "But yeah, sure, why not? I've been really dying to try that label."

"Great! I should be done here in the next hour or so. You're welcome to stay and wait while I close down...or meet up later?"

"I can hang around. I don't have anything going on. Can I grab a hot toddy with Buffalo Trace in the meantime?"

"Coming right up!"

***

As we walked the short distance back to my place after I locked up The Bubble, she still had a somber, timid air about her. She seemed so distraught; I honestly just didn't want her to be alone for the night. I poured two whiskeys, and we sat on the couch. She took in my apartment, with its minimal decorations and personal curated pieces like my old Victrola record player and the frame that held a picture of my entire family, which included me, my mom, and my brother.

"Do they live around here?" She nodded towards the frame.

"Yeah, my mom is in the next town over, and Smith is an airline pilot. He lives in Massachusetts. We all get together twice a month. But I visit my mom at least once a week to bring over groceries and check in on her." I took this as an opening to get more information about her. "What about you? Do you have family nearby?"

"No, actually. I've never been to this part of the country. My family is all out west, but I lived in Boston shortly before moving here. I thought Boston was going to be the place for me but then I was proved wrong."

Oh no, she was starting to do that mile-long stare-off-into-the-distance thing again. "Aw well, Boston is a busy place for sure. I always feel like there's way too much going on there. And the traffic! Don't even get me started."

"Haha, yeah," she faltered. And then she seemed to snap out of it. "So, what are your thoughts on the Antique 107?"

"It's great! Very smooth, a little bit of a bite but not nearly as sharp as Evan Williams or Jack Daniels," I responded.

She giggled, lightly. "I agree." Her laugh was infectious. "So, what about movies? Any favorites?" she asked.

"You know, I actually haven't had much time to watch any lately, with the holidays and work being so busy. Mind if we throw one on now?" I asked.

"Sounds good! I like drama, suspense, and thrillers."

"Alright, let's see what we have here." As I navigated to Netflix, we bantered back and forth about different movie options for a while, before settling on a light-hearted drama we both hadn't seen.

About twenty minutes in, I glanced over at Sofia, who was sound asleep, her whiskey already gone. I threw a blanket over her and got myself ready to get some sleep in my own bed. In the morning I would ask if she wanted to grab a coffee at Kyla's.

***

I woke to the faintest sound of footsteps going downstairs, and the front door to the old house closing ever so quietly. I figured it must have been my neighbor, always early to rise for her morning run or trip to the local coffee shop. I got up shortly afterwards and looked out the window but didn't see anyone, just footsteps in the fresh layer of overnight frost. It was already 8:00 A.M. I ventured out to the living room to ask Sofia how she slept but she was nowhere to be found. How strange, I pondered. I went to grab a glass of water from the kitchen. As I was pouring the glass from the tap, I noticed the sapphire ring was gone. Not only had the ring disappeared, so had Sofia.

I guess sometimes extraordinary things prefer not to be found.

Roselyn Peterson, PhD, has published over 40 peer-reviewed scientific research manuscripts. This is her first foray into fiction writing. She plans to continue writing in both arenas and is excited to continue Elliott and Sofia's story. She lives with her soon-to-be husband Rob and black kitty Melli in Rhode Island.

A Total Eclipse of the Heart

— Kara Marziali

"You are simply extraordinary, Ann," Guy said in a faux British accent, masking his own foreign dialect.

"Do you mean *ex-straw-din-airy* meaning exceptional, or do you mean *extra-ordinary*, as in exceptionally common?"

Guy laughed and held up his glass as if to toast her. "You are very funny, Ann." She was not trying to be funny. She was just trying to be real and get through this date unscathed.

Ann and Guy were sharing a wild mushroom and fig pizza at The Gilded Palette, a trendy restaurant in the heart of New Rochelle's Arts District known for its culturally diverse food and handcrafted cocktails. The multi-story restored historic building had been renovated by a group of innovative millennials with a penchant for fusion cuisine and historic preservation. Guy suggested dinner after their visit to the Thomas Paine Cottage. Ann had taken students on field trips to the museum in years past, but her visit to the homestead was far more enjoyable with Guy.

"When Thomas Paine wrote *Common Sense,* he was an obscure immigrant," Ann said, pointing to a replica of the document. "Then in January of 1776, this small pamphlet helped to ignite the flame of independence in America!"

"As an immigrant to the US, that gives me hope." Guy's smile animated his whole face and generated creases that framed his expressive eyes.

"Why? Are you planning on starting a revolution?" Ann teased.

"No, the only thing I'd like to plan is another date with you. Let's discuss our next adventure. How about axe throwing or an escape room?"

Ann considered Guy's suggestions. She told him that she'd never participated in either activity but would be open to both. What she didn't tell him was that in her mind she had already survived the greatest escape of all - an unhealthy marriage.

It had been four years since her divorce. Dale had moved on quickly, as she assumed he would. The breakup was so cliché. Husband cheats on wife and runs off with his secretary who is half his age. Ann was left with the house, a Netflix subscription, and plenty of resentments. At the time, she was an empty nester hoping to retire early. Instead, she was still teaching English literature to central-city teens who think Chaucer is a shallow dish on which a cup is placed.

Ann was sitting in the teachers' lounge poking at her lunch with a flimsy metal fork. "I think the cafeteria menu has reached an all-time low. Why would they name a menu item after the school mascot? Bengal Bites is nothing more than rocks covered in gravy. I feel sick." She wanted to blame her condition on the food in front of her, but the truth was, Ann had been wallowing in self-pity for weeks. "I am sick and tired of my life," she announced to Janelle, who had been her co-worker and lunch companion for the past 12 years. "I have absolutely nothing to look forward to. Nothing remarkable happens to me." Ann sighed. "Even my name is commonplace."

"You're teaching *Hamlet* at a public high school. What could be more exciting than that?" Janelle said sarcastically. She was more than just a colleague; she'd been Ann's support and sidekick through the most challenging times. "You should start dating, Ann."

"No way."

"Why not? It's time for you to meet someone special. Someone who treats you like the gem you are."

And that's how it started. That evening, after Ann corrected student essays, she wrote her profile for Destiny's Door, a new dating app for singles over 50. Her first attempts were clumsy and unskilled. Despite earning an undergraduate degree in English, she had no words to describe who she was or what she wanted. Dale had been her first and only boyfriend, so she felt unqualified to write a personal statement about matters of the heart.

Besides, she thought, who would want a sarcastic, post-menopausal divorced woman with little hope for romance? Maybe she would forget about the dating site and get a mid-life tattoo, go sky-diving, or undergo a cosmetic procedure. After two glasses of wine, she decided the cheapest and most practical option was to finish writing the profile.

> *I am a considerate and scholarly woman seeking the companionship of a gentleman. I am looking for a relationship that is fun without being sophomoric; intellectually stimulating without being stuffy; flirty not dirty; warm not smothering; earnest but filled with lots of laughter; and attentive with ample room for alone time. If you are someone who is harmonious, humorous, handsome, helpful, honest, happy-go-lucky, hardworking, healthy, huggable, and high-spirited, I would enjoy getting to know you.*

For the past year, she'd gone out socially with dozens of men she'd met online. Most dates were futile appointments held at popular and pricey coffee houses with the remote possibility of a subsequent date.

There was Jerry, who brought a background check and proof of his good driving record because, as he put it, "you never know who you're meeting on the Internet." During this encounter, Ann felt like a hiring manager rather than a would-be girlfriend.

Kevin was a "bah-tend-uh" who spoke with a recognizable and offensive Boston accent. He was "wicked excited" to meet Ann and bragged about his "cah covered with bumpah stickahs."

The date with Eric, age 58, seemed promising at first. That is, until he admitted to lying about his name, age, occupation, and his marital status. In actuality, he was Ernie - a jobless 63-year-old who lived with his mother.

Rob, a financial advisor, had a popular YouTube channel. He contributed to a weekly vlog entitled "Future Funded." Ann admitted she didn't know much about investing, and Rob admitted he didn't know much about Shakespeare. When the date ended, the biggest yield was a mutual agreement that there really wasn't much in common between them.

After 45 minutes of listening to Mike, a plumber, blather about copper piping, valves, elbows and tees, Ann was certain the idea of "coupling" was out of the question.

And there was the one guy who, upon learning that Ann taught English lit, boasted about the size of his "Charles Dickens."

But Guy was different. There was an air of intrigue about him, as if he'd leapt off the pages of a book. Guy was exceptionally ob-servant like Sherlock Holmes, dapper like Jay Gatsby, introverted like Fitzwilliam Darcy, and he enjoyed his martinis like James Bond—shaken, not stirred.

He grew up in Monaco and emigrated to the US 22 years ago to take a job with IBM in New York. Ann learned from Guy's profile he was widowed at age 35. His wife died of cancer when their two boys were still in primary school. Guy raised them with the help of an au pair they called "Nou-nou." Both his adult sons live in Europe, and he visits them every few years.

"Now that you know so much about me, please tell me more about you." Before picking up another slice of pizza, Guy made a passing gesture with his hand, which meant it was now Ann's turn to be transparent and vulnerable.

Ann was trying to channel Katness Everdeen, Jo March, and Nancy Drew, but she felt more like Bridget Jones. "There's not much to tell. I lead a very boring life. I teach English lit to hormonal teen-agers; my ex left me for a bimbo named Tiffany; I am a Scorpio, which is probably why I tend to be sardonic; my middle name is Louise, after my grandmother; I've never eaten jellied eels but noticed them on the menu; and when I was seven, a neighborhood dog named Pinky bit me here." Ann stretched her right arm toward Guy, showing off the still-noticeable scar on the fleshy part of her hand between her thumb and index finger.

Guy lowered his reading glasses onto the bridge of his nose, peered at the cicatrix on Ann's hand, and kissed it.

"Ann, I like you a lot, so whether it's me or some other guy - and I hope it's me - please don't ever settle. You are an amazing woman. You are lovely to look at, quick witted, independent. And brilliant, which is super sexy to me."

Their dates continued in this fashion, and Ann found herself spending more and more time with Guy. Meeting for coffee at Star-bucks. Walking in a dog park even though neither of them had a dog. Visits to the athenaeum, a comedy club, or an outdoor flea market.

Dinner at her place, a card game at his. Pumpkin picking. Leaf peeping. And while the weather was getting colder, her affection for him grew hotter.

In December, Guy surprised Ann with tickets to New York City Ballet's "The Nutcracker." After the performance, they walked, arm in arm, humming the memorable melody of Tchaikovsky's March. Ann stopped to admire a window display with its twinkling lights and festive Christmas decorations. While she was looking at some hand-blown glass ornaments, she felt Guy staring intently at her.

"What?" she said, feeling self-conscious.

"Santa brought me an early present, and it's you," Guy said as he leaned in closer. Ann was nervous and she clumsily turned her head away because she honestly wasn't sure if she remembered how to kiss. Dale had stopped kissing Ann shortly after the birth of their son, and she was too infatuated with the baby to notice. Until it was too late. By then she had discovered Dale was cheating on her, and she pretended not to know.

But that was then. This moment was different. Ann was with Guy now, and she wanted desperately to send him a sign of her desire. The chemistry between them was palpable. She tilted her chin and directed her eyes toward him. Guy responded by brushing her cheek with the back of his hand. And then, he gently pressed his lips to hers. Their first kiss was magical, and Ann couldn't wait to tell Janelle once they got back from winter break.

***

"I have never felt like this before, Janelle. Guy is…" Ann searched for the words as she shuffled papers. "He's intelligent and refined. He's got a great sense of humor, and he's sooo thoughtful."

"Ann, you are all those things, too. Smart, cultured, funny, kind. So why shouldn't you be with someone perfectly suited for you? This is what you've been waiting for."

"I can really be myself with him and when we're together, I feel so, so happy." Ann stood up and all but skipped down the hall to her next class. She was looking forward to discussing Jane Eyre with her students that afternoon.

Guy's profession as a security engineer for a leading technology company required him to be analytical, proactive, detail-oriented, inquisitive, dependable, composed, and serious. With Ann, however, he let his guard down and showed a softer side. He was passionate, gracious, and droll. He brought her flowers, held her hand, and flattered her often. More than once, he called her extraordinary.

"No, I'm really quite *ordinary*. The only thing *extra* about me is the weight around my mid-section."

Guy laughed again, and Ann chuckled, too. Their conversations flowed so easily, a first for Ann. She had felt so uptight and uneasy in her marriage to Dale. And her initial jaunt on to the dating scene was equally uncomfortable.

"Seriously. I'm just your average middle-aged divorcee," she said trying to feign modesty. "What I mean to say is, I've come to terms with the fact that my life doesn't need to be filled with anything remarkable. I'll never grace the cover of *Vogue*, achieve a groundbreaking scientific discovery, or perform an act of incredible heroism. Heck, I may not even witness a breathtaking natural phenomenon."

"So how about we change all of that, Ann." Guy reached across the table to take her hand. "There's a particular natural phenomenon I'd like to experience with you."

Ann's face flushed at the hint of something erotic. "That sounds like a double entendre."

"Oh, you're terrible. That was *not* a sexual inuendo. I was referring to the total solar eclipse happening next April."

Six months later, Ann and Guy were planning a trip to the Adirondacks to witness the rare event of the moon passing between the sun and Earth.

"There are phases in a total solar eclipse," Guy began. "The first contact is when the moon becomes visible over the sun's disk, and it looks like the moon has taken a little bite out of the sun. The second contact is when the moon covers the entire disk of the sun. This is such a dramatic stage of a total solar eclipse. The sky goes dark, temperatures fall, and birds and animals go quiet. Talk about extraordinary!"

Ann hung on his every word as Guy continued to describe the event. "The third contact occurs when the moon starts moving away, and the sun reappears. And finally, the fourth contact is when the eclipse ends. The moon disappears and the sun is fully visible again."

"It seems to me that an eclipse - when the sun is blocked and the landscape plunges into temporary obscurity - is a metaphor for life. That despite darkness, the light will return."

"Precisely."

The day before the total solar eclipse, Ann and Guy drove to Westport, NY, a charming town nestled on the shores of Lake Champlain. Their ride was picturesque and pleasant. They took turns pointing out the natural beauty of the Adirondack Mountains along the way. The dialogue between them was carefree and punctuated by laughter. When they weren't discussing current events, gallery exhibits, or telling tales from their childhood, they were singing 80s music and quizzing each other about pop stars.

Earlier in the week during a lunch break, Janelle had interrogated Ann about her upcoming trip with Guy. "What is the dress code for a total solar eclipse? Are you outside the *whole* time? What will the temperature be like? Does it really get that dark? Like nighttime?" Janelle asked in rapid fire. Then she nestled her fork on the side of her salad plate, paused, and said, "Ann, I am *really* excited for you."

Ann had also stopped eating. She had been through so much over the past few years. The divorce and emotional numbness amid the shock of it all. Anger directed at her former spouse and eventually herself. The loneliness relieved only by retail therapy, a bubble bath, a call from Janelle, the *New York Times* crossword, her beatnik Manhattan shrink, or an occasional glass of merlot. Then acceptance. She woke up one day and realized that divorcing Dale was the most liberating thing she'd ever done. For the first time as an adult woman, Ann was standing in her own sovereignty and gaining some agency over her life. Once she shattered the faulty belief that she was too old for romance, she was able to move on. When she met Guy, she discovered she could still create deep connections with others and fulfill the fundamental human need for intimacy.

Lots of people were captivated by the spectacular celestial event of the total solar eclipse on April 8, 2024, but it was especially meaningful for Ann. She wrote in her journal:

> *Westport has been a quaint and quiet Adirondack town, until today. Throngs of people have flocked here to get a glimpse of the solar eclipse. The locals have been welcoming us and undoubtedly appreciate the boost to the economy. Guy and I stopped at the gourmet cheese shop to pick up a wedge of aged Gruyère, a baguette, some red grapes and 2 bottles of Perrier before walking toward Ballard Park.*
>
> *Guy set up his camera while I laid out a blanket and arranged our picnic lunch. Other travelers arrived, looking for a viewing spot,*

and the hum of excitement was evident. Even though the sun was shining, there was a chilling breeze coming off Lake Champlain, so I was glad I brought a sweatshirt with me. Guy noted how similar the pattern on the plaid blanket was to the flannel shirt he was wearing. (Clearly, we both have a thing for buffalo check!)

In the distance, we heard music. Then the vocals of three rambunctious teenagers drowned out the distinctive rasp of Bonnie Tyler's "Total Eclipse of the Heart." I opened the sparkling water, made a toast to Guy, looked into his slate-blue eyes, and sang along. ("Every now and then, I know there's no one in the universe as magical and wondrous as youuuu...") Guy joined in moments later and we erupted in giggles over the amusement of this shared experience.

We made small talk with a young couple running after a toddler who innocently made her way onto our blanket. When Guy offered the little girl a piece of bread, she looked to her parents for approval, made herself comfortable on the blanket next to Guy, and made "yummy sounds" while she ate. After they left, I remembered my own experiences as a new mom and shared them with Guy.

When the time drew near for the eclipse, I unearthed two pairs of protective glasses from my tote bag and handed one pair to Guy. He plopped them on his head, so they'd be ready to lower at a moment's notice and he winked at me. There was a noticeable hush in the crowd. I kept glancing at my watch to check the time. I guess I was afraid I would somehow miss the occurrence, and Guy gently teased me about my fastidiousness.

Then, as if midnight was mistaken for midday, the sky began to darken. The moon drifted purposefully in front of the sun and in a matter of minutes, we were enveloped in inky blackness. I *wasn't aware that my mouth fell open in astonishment, and before I realized it, Guy's tongue entered the small space where my lips parted. When the kiss was over, I said, "I'm crazy about you."*

Love is a lot like the once-in-a-lifetime experience of a cosmic interlude. When you find it, appreciate it, attach meaning to it, and cherish it. Revel in the rarity of it and when it takes your breath away, remember the rest of the world is also in awe.

When Ann got back to school the following day, she felt renewed and giddy.

"So, tell me *everything*," Janelle squeezed Ann's arm and pushed her into an empty classroom.

Ann shared the highlights of the trip before the homeroom bell rang. "For the past several months, I've been having so much fun. Getting to know that man, this *Guy*. Going on picnics, enjoying the symphony and museums, talking for hours on end over the phone."

"Would you say life is no longer predictable?" Janelle said, leaning on one of the student desks.

"Are you kidding? My life is a-ma-zing!" Ann tossed her head back. "Jan, I am in love. But I also rediscovered myself. My ordinary moments are infused with a sense of magic and purpose. I feel as if I've been pulled from my mundane existence into something special."

"Sooo, is this like happily ever after and ride off into the sunset?"

"You know, I used to think that everything needed to be planned out so perfectly. I used to want 'forever.' These days, I think in terms of 'for now.'"

There didn't need to be anything more. Ann smiled and knew, with Guy by her side, the best was yet to come. And it would be *extraordinary*.

Kara Marziali is the author of *Kara Koala and Her Kaleidoscope of Feelings* and its accompanying activity book and journal. She is featured in three other ARIA anthologies and was a regular columnist for a local newspaper. In addition to her role as a writer, she teaches dramatic literature, theatre, and art at the Osher Lifelong Learning Institute at URI. She also serves as the artist-in-residence at Wood River Health, offering creative outlets to help people with their well-being. She is most comfortable in environments that stimulate curiosity, cultivate creativity, kindle compassion, and facilitate connections.

The Gifts of Grace

— *Douglas S. Levine*

"Rack 'em up!" Jake whooped. "You're hot tonight, Bryce! But *when* you run the table again, I'll have to claim your pool stick and give someone else a chance, hotshot." Jake smiled like a Cheshire cat, delighted with the party planner's arrangements for the evening's festivities, and rooted for his older brother. "Go get 'em, big bro!"

Bryce had other distractions to choose from if Jake's prediction held up. Jake rented the American Legion Riverside Post hall to celebrate. "*You are hereby SUMMONED...*" his invitation read, "*... to join Dawn and me in mourning at her Past-Her-Prime 30th Birthday Extravaganza on February 20, 2002. Hold the date!*" Rather ironic, Bryce thought. One had to know these junior folk to get the joke. Dawn went along with the plans for the carnival-like setting and apparatus the party consultant secured at Jake's request. As the pool balls were racked, Bryce observed the exuberance at the slot, pinball, and Skee-Ball machines, Cornhole boards, magnetic darts booths, ping pong tables, and bar. He understood why Jake was jacked up by the scene.

After he chalked his cue, Bryce's break shot elicited applause after four balls rattled into the corner and side pockets. He was in a transcendent realm, where his mind expanded beyond earthly limits and was simultaneously concentrated on cue stick, cue ball, and target, and shot after shot, ball after ball fell into a pocket.

Bryce was capable at most games, a way to relax with his family between his shifts in the emergency room. For years, pool had been his favorite pastime, an obsession, perhaps a subconscious quest. When he played pool, he hoped some hint might emerge in his altered consciousness and lead him to the answer to his penultimate question: *How ...?* That notion was reinforced when he sighted a particular ball on the baize, the green, felt-like cloth that covered the table's playing surface. If, per Jake's game rules, Bryce sank that last ball and cleaned the pool table, he would be required to interrupt his inner journey and relinquish his pool stick and place at the table to another celebrant.

The last of the fifteen numbered, color-coded balls—a beacon beckoning Bryce to the past—lay four hands from the nearest pocket. He scrutinized the solid black ball and marveled at its significance. As he took a deep breath, he reentered the ethereal zone and lined up and savored his final stroke at the cue ball for the night. Before he pulled the stick back to shoot, his trance was broken by Meg: his wife and the greatest gift and gem of his life, the miraculous manifestation of questions he posed decades before, mother of their two children, and chief operating officer of the non-profit pediatric hospital. Her timing was perfect; she had walked over after she paused her chat with Dawn to watch him. Meg bore a smile twice as wide as Jake's and gazed into Bryce's eyes, her signal of encouragement. He acknowledged her sign with a wink and a head nod and confidently knocked the mysterious and unpredictable eight ball into the corner pocket.

* * *

How was it possible to remember smells? Bryce's recent favorites were Meg's perfume, their morning medium roast coffee, their kids' peanut butter, and his barbecue sauce. But one particular aroma, the scent of Crayola crayons, had been with him since 1964, when he was four years old. The assortment of colorful wax markers was a present from his older sister. She demonstrated how to use them, warned him not to eat them, and advised him to draw on paper or in coloring books after she inspected, smirked at, and wiped his master-piece off her bedroom wall. She did not yell at Bryce. Never did. When he was older and traded stories with his friends about their respective siblings, he learned they would have killed to have had a sister like Grace. Bryce's memories of growing up on Bullocks Point Avenue were ensconced in their parents' love and its sustenance as he entered and traversed adulthood. How fortunate he was to have Grace who loved, taught, and guided him, too. He believed she pre-pared for the role of big sister for the entirety of her nine years before he was born.

The crayons entertained Bryce, but these provoked unrealistic expectations. Grace found pages of his art discarded willy nilly in her bedroom. "What's wrong with these?" she asked.

"I don't like them. I started over," Bryce grumbled as he scribbled with a red crayon with enough force to break it in half. He slumped his shoulders and groaned.

Two days later, Grace presented him with an Etch a Sketch and a can of Play-Doh purchased by their parents on her recommenda-tion. "When you draw or make sculptures, these are easier if you want to start over," she said. "I'll show you how they work." Bryce beamed with delight as he experimented with the knobs on the magic screen and created his first forms with the modeling clay.

When Bryce was ready to try architecture and engineering, Grace introduced him to Lincoln Logs and the Erector Set, courtesy of Grace's lobbying of their parents. Brother and sister absorbed themselves in construction projects on weekends and weekday afternoons after Grace returned home from school. Their collection of games diversified to include Slinky, G.I. Joe, Mr. Potato Head, and Cootie. Bryce favored unusual, anatomically incorrect configurations of Mr. Potato Head and Cootie, and he liked to bomb the soldier, tater, and bug with Play-Doh munitions, all in playful fun. Grace celebrated each of Bryce's maneuvers, and he relished her attention. What Bryce liked best was that he could talk with Grace and ask her any conceivable question while they played together or watched television. Especially when they watched perplexing TV shows like *The Smothers Brothers Comedy Hour* and *Car 54, Where Are You?*

When Bryce was six, Grace furnished him with a football and a helmet that spawned the endearing nickname she would forever use for him. Indifferent to the rules that governed how the sport was played, Bryce took to bulldozing Grace's hollow core bedroom door, ball tucked in an armpit and helmeted head down, to produce a *THUD!* that reverberated throughout the house. Among the monikers Grace might have chosen for her little brother—Slinky Stinky, G.I. Shmo, Mr. Spud, or Cootie Cutie, as inspired by the toys, or Yo-Yo Man, Toody, or Muldoon, as influenced by two of the TV shows they watched together—she selected Bonehead. Grace would be concentrating on her homework when a *THUD!* echoed behind her, Bryce's calling card. "That must be my brother, Bryce! Come in, *Bonehead.*"

At age seven, Bryce's new game was Spy. He had not abandoned helmet-butting Grace's door, but Spy provided a more subtle form of entertainment that gave him the opportunity to gain a mastery of imperceptibility. The quarry for his espionage was Grace, but only if her door was wide open or ajar with enough space for him to look through. When there wasn't a slit to peek past, Bryce religiously adhered to his sister's request. "When my door is open, you can come in. But if it's shut, please knock or *THUD!* and I'll tell you if the coast is clear. Okay, *Bonehead?*" Grace said nothing about snooping if her door was in a position to invite secret surveillance.

Spy enlightened Bryce about high school girls' doings: write cards and letters or scribe in a diary. Read a book while pacing about the room or sitting cross-legged on the floor. Listen to music or sports on the radio. Peruse and select clothing from the closet and chest of drawers. Adjust strings on a tennis racket. Roll out a mat and perform weird feats of flexibility while standing or kneeling on it. Brush hair while meditating before a mirror. Stand as still as a statue and stare out the window.

In addition to Grace's odd form of exercise, another of her habits puzzled Bryce. On occasion, she took a black ball from her bookshelf, sat on the floor, whispered to it, shook it, examined it, and either laughed or sighed as she replaced the article. One day, Bryce's curiosity overwhelmed his devotion to the practices of silence and invisibility that Spy demanded, and he barged in. "What are you doing?" he asked.

"Getting advice," she said.

"About what?"

"Well, *Bonehead*. That's private."

"How does that thing give advice?" asked Bryce.

"That thing," Grace said as she retrieved it, "is the Magic 8 Ball. I'll show you how it works. First, I have to ask it a question." She and Bryce sat on the floor with the sphere between them. Grace wiggled her fingers at the ball and asked, "Should my brother and I to go to

Cresent Park today?" She picked it up, shook it, turned it upside down, and handed it to Bryce. "Read the Magic 8 Ball's advice, its answer to my question."

Yes.

Grace said, "Looks like we should get ready to go to the amusement park."

"Yay!" Bryce laughed. "Can I ask the Magic 8 Ball a question?"

"You mean, *may* I ask the Magic 8 Ball a question?"

"Yeah." Bryce feigned defeat in the game of Grammar that Grace always won. "May I?"

"I think I should ask the oracle." Grace took the ball from her brother, set it on the floor, and wiggled her fingers at it. "Is Bryce ready to ask the all-knowing Magic 8 Ball a question now?" She shook the ball, turned it upside down, and showed her brother the answer.

Very doubtful.

That time, Bryce's expression of disappointment was sincere. "Don't be sad, Bryce. I'm going to give you the Magic 8 Ball when you turn eight in a couple of months. Right before I go to college. I'll write out instructions for how to use it. *The rules are very important!* We'll read them together, and you'll be ready to ask the eight ball questions. I promise. But for now, let's go to the park. Do you want to ride the carousel? And get ice cream?"

Grace kept her promises. Bryce would wait to ask questions of the irresistible sphere when she was not home to answer them. The Magic 8 Ball faded from his imagination as he contemplated a merry-go-round and a chocolate ice cream cone.

When Grace was out of the house and not available for Spy, Bryce wandered into her bedroom and approached her bookshelf, mesmerized by the Magic 8 Ball. What was inside it? How did it know how to answer questions? Could it predict the future? Was its advice always right? Bryce wanted to query the ball, but he resisted taking it from the shelf to examine it and ask crucial questions, perhaps some he did not want to ask Grace. Like with their games, Grace would show him how to use the Magic 8 Ball. He could wait because soon, he would turn eight.

The evening before his birthday, Bryce roamed into Grace's room. She was away with classmates at a party before she moved into a dormitory later that week and started classes at URI. Many of her friends would leave East Providence to go to different colleges, too, and the homies wanted to celebrate together for a last time. While Bryce pondered the allure of institutions of higher learning, another one of his growing list of questions, he inspected the Magic 8 Ball and tabulated the hours until it would be his.

Before he counted to eight, Bryce was alerted by flashing lights outside Grace's window. Two police officers exited their vehicle and walked to his home's front entrance. When Bryce heard the doorbell, he scampered to the landing at the head of the stairs and saw his parents open the door to admit a woman and man in uniform. The four adults spoke in hushed tones at the entryway for several minutes before Bryce's mother cried and embraced his father. Bryce thought the Magic 8 Ball had bestowed its powers of prognostication on him: he knew he would never see Grace again. Never play with her again. Never talk with her and ask her questions again.

Bryce's birthday party was postponed until after Grace's funeral, an arrangement his parents discussed with him and which he accepted. He was old enough to be more upset about the loss of his big sister in a car crash than a belated party with birthday cake and presents. Of all the gifts he might have wanted, he was most eager to get the Magic 8 Ball, not because of its knowledge and power but because it was Grace's. He sorely missed her.

Several days after Grace's funeral, Bryce gained the courage to enter Grace's room. She always welcomed him to visit her and did not mind him coming in when she was not there. But that was when she was alive. Was it all right to be there when she was…wherever she was? He knew she wanted him to have the Magic 8 Ball, which justified his return to her room. He walked to the bookshelf, found an envelope under the ball with *Bryce* written on it, opened the envelope, and pulled out a page with his sister's handwriting:

Magic 8 Ball Rules:
1. DO NOT throw or roll the 8 Ball.
2. DO NOT drop the 8 Ball.
3. DO NOT take a bath or shower with or submerge the 8 Ball. DO
   NOT get it wet!
4. DO NOT try to open the 8 Ball.
5. DO NOT move the 8 Ball unless you have a question to ask it.
6. Ask the 8 Ball questions that are answered yes or no, shake it, turn
   it upside down, and read its answer.
7. DO NOT get mad at the 8 Ball, no matter what it says.
8. WISELY choose the question you ask the 8 Ball.
9. DO NOT be a bonehead with the 8 Ball, Bonehead!
10. ALWAYS TRUST in the wisdom of the Magic 8 Ball.

Bryce giggled. He laughed whenever Grace called him Bonehead. And he thought he understood the rules. If he became confused by any of them, he would seek clarification from the ball. He had an important question to ask. He sat on the floor, placed the Magic 8

Ball before him, wiggled his fingers at it, asked, "Is Grace in heaven?" and shook the ball.

Yes – definitely.

Bryce rested easier. Grace was a good person. A sensational big sister. She belonged in heaven. The ball's response provoked another question. "Can I…oops, *may* I ask *Grace* questions?"

Concentrate and ask again.

How long to wait? Would this ball with an eight cooperate and give clear answers? He counted to one hundred and asked, "*Can Grace answer my questions?*"

Better not tell you now.

Bryce sighed. Was his choice of questions unwise, in defiance of Grace's eighth rule? And how well would he abide by all ten of her instructions? Bryce took the Magic 8 Ball and the list of rules to his room, placed them on his desk, and postponed his interrogation because the oracle's advice might have further tried his patience.

As Bryce grew older, the Magic 8 Ball became a loving memento of Grace and a confidante with which he would only ask the wisest of questions. "Do I really have to study for tomorrow's geography test?"

Without a doubt.

Bryce wanted to watch TV instead of poring over boring maps. "Won't I pass with what I've learned?"

Don't count on it.

Bryce glared at the ball. Its answers were much like what Grace would have said. "Is Grace answering my questions?"

Ask again later.

"Argh! You're no help." Bryce was about to seize the ball but grew contrite when he recalled Rule 7: *DO NOT get mad at the 8 Ball, no matter what it says.*

Bryce's interest in games had evolved to sports when he entered East Providence High, but these were less important than his homework because of the Magic 8 Ball's guidance. He was blessed with talent to make any of the school's athletic squads, but he wanted to play only one team sport to limit disruption of his studies. "Am I good enough to try out for varsity basketball?"

Most likely.

"That doesn't sound like a ringing endorsement, Mr. 8 Ball. Is baseball *more* likely, wise guy?"

It is certain.

Bryce lettered as the team's shortstop and was integral to the Townies' winning seasons. He sustained good grades and made honor roll every school term.

When Bryce was a senior, he turned to the Magic 8 Ball for crucial advice. "Corinne is nice. Should I ask her to the prom?"

My reply is no.

"Yikes. We had so much fun at the movies. She was my first choice. How about Kimberly?"

Outlook not so good.

"Oh, you malevolent 8 Ball! You are full of unwelcome news. What am I supposed to do?" Bryce did not expect a response; the ball irritated and baffled him. *Both* Corinne and Kim would turn him down? *Gee whiz.* Who else could he ask? Who...? Who...? *Her?* Schoolmates since first grade. Valentines as kids. Competitors in Debate Club who learned from each other. Lab partners in chemistry...and he *so* lucked out because she was a genius. "Maybe...Meg?"

As I see it, yes.

Was it Meg's prom gown, Bryce's tuxedo, the corsage, their shared past and mutual respect, the music and dancing, or the Magic

8 Ball that cast the die on prom night? Meg and Bryce became inseparable sweethearts. They attended Roger Williams College and got engaged before the start of their senior year. They would marry after they completed their respective phases of education: business administration for Meg, medical school for Bryce.

The Magic 8 Ball became Bryce's talisman, the source of his good luck in life. His reminder to follow the rules. He missed Grace but was a beneficiary of her love and care and the heir to her magic sphere that knew the future and gave profound advice. Bryce never felt so high on life until he connected with Meg in their new relationship and anticipated matrimonial bliss. Until Meg's symptoms started. She became perpetually tired and lost weight. She drenched her night clothes and bedsheets in sweat at night. Bryce detected the swellings in Meg's neck when he caressed her. She needed to see a *real* doctor.

"Can you…" Meg began to ask as soon as Bryce picked up the phone. Her coughing interrupted her question. "…please come over?"

Bryce worried Meg had news that was far worse than what the Magic 8 Ball occasionally doled out. He closed his textbook and dashed out to drive to Meg's apartment. When he arrived, she hugged him and led him to a couch in her studio where they sat side by side.

"The doctors found out what's wrong," she said. "I can be treated, but…"

"What's wrong?" Bryce asked. "Whatever it is, we'll get through it together."

Meg grimaced. "They said I have a type of blood cancer." She paused and held Bryce's intent look for several moments. "It's non-Hodgkin lymphoma. You've learned about it in school?"

Bryce had begun clinical rotations and met patients in the hospital and clinic as an apprentice to the med school graduates in residency training and supervising physicians who were responsible for care decisions. He was taught to be objective and dispassionate, to intellectualize when he took medical histories and performed physical examinations on patients who could be horribly ill. Often, there were treatment options, medications, sometimes surgery. Other times, only supportive, comfort care could be provided to alleviate symptoms because there was nothing else that could be done to avert disease progression, complications, and death. Because of the last, Bryce's heart was pierced, his head spun, and his gut wrenched as he listened to Meg and tried to put on a brave face. "Yes. But please tell me what the doctors said?"

"There's treatment. Drugs. Maybe radiation. They said they can't make guarantees, but my chances to live, to survive, are pretty good. It's just…" Meg covered her face with her hands and Bryce gathered her in his arms.

"It will be okay, Meg. I love you. I'm here. Our families and friends will be, too."

Meg pulled away. "There are side effects *with* the treatments."

"I know." Bryce was aware of the physical and symptomatic reactions to cancer chemotherapy and radiation treatment. "But Meg. They're temporary. Unpleasant, but manageable. And you're tough."

Meg dabbed her eyes with a tissue. "I'll be able to take the stomach upset. Diarrhea. Hair loss. I'm already dealing with fevers and fatigue. The doctors said the same thing as you. The side effects during treatment are a small price to pay. It's just…"

Bryce could not read what Meg's eyes expressed. "Just what, Meg? You can tell me."

Meg swallowed. "There can be long-term side effects *after* I'm done with the treatments. The drugs and radiation can mess up my eggs. We might not be able to get pregnant. I know how much you want kids. Like me. But that might not be in the cards." Meg embraced Bryce. When she pulled away, she placed her engagement ring in Bryce's hand.

"What? No. Meg, I love you. We'll do this together. I don't understand."

"Dear Bryce. I'm not saying I don't want to marry you. I just don't know. This lymphoma. The uncertainty. It's so confusing. So much." Meg stood and walked to the other side of the room and turned to face Bryce. "Let's postpone. See how things go. I think we can and should slow down. Give us time to decide," Meg said.

"I don't want to not marry—"

"I know. But you might think differently. The news is fresh. You deserve time to digest it, like me. I'm not saying goodbye. I love you and want your support. But think. Talk to family and friends. And time will tell. For both of us. We both have choices." Meg walked back to Bryce, hugged him, and led him to the door.

Bryce felt lost. How could this happen? He and Meg were kind people. They followed the rules. Worked hard in school. They were succeeding. They knew they were meant for each other and… it felt like the rules were being broken. He followed Meg's advice and sought counsel.

"We know you love Meg," Bryce's mom said. "She wants you to take stock because of her illness. She wants to be fair and for you to be clear in your mind about what you want to do."

Bryce's dad said, "I don't envy you. No one wants to be in this situation. You know your heart and it's all right to balance that with what's in your head. What you have learned."

Bryce would not burden his little brother. Jake adored Meg, and Bryce had not told him she was sick. Bryce's friends offered conflicting suggestions:

"…besides, there are plenty of other fish in the sea…"

"…you made a commitment. The honorable thing to do is to keep it…"

"…you deserve the chance to have a normal life and can…"

"…and heck. Doesn't love conquer all?"

"…but she's not obligating you. You can walk away or stay friends or…"

"…the doctors said there are no guarantees. What about the flip side? That she *will* live and *will* be able to have kids?"

"…and what rule says you *have* to go through with it? She returned your ring and…"

Bryce's parents would not tell him what to do, but his friends were willing to dispense advice that was sugar-coated, simple-minded, or downright discouraging. He knew he could not put a decision about sustaining his engagement to Meg up for a vote. Only he could decide. But how? What did Meg want, *really* want? What did *he* really want? He wanted Meg's cancer cured. But what about kids? Would they change their minds? Would they opt to adopt? Might they? His questions persisted.

Bryce wished he could talk to Grace. Of everyone he knew, she would be the one and only soul who would know what he should do and tell him. He picked up the Magic 8 Ball and asked, "May I ask Grace a question?"

Reply hazy, try again.

Bryce gritted his teeth and tried once more. "May I *please* ask Grace a *very* important question?"

Cannot predict now.

Bryce prayed the Magic 8 Ball would help him decide what to do. He retrieved Grace's list of rules and read them through, one by one, once. Twice. Three times. *Rules!* Why all the rules? He expected a life with Meg. *Normal* was supposed to be the rule. Health. Happiness. But the rules for having these things in life were broken all the time. He knew from what happened to Grace. He knew from medical school and patients. About genes and inherited susceptibilities to certain diseases. About bad luck. Health and normalcy were not guaranteed for everyone all the time. If the rules were broken for Meg and Bryce—by what? Nature? Could he break the rules, too? Was that not his right? Was breaking the rules part of the rules?

Bryce shook with anticipation when he decided to ignore one of Meg's instructions for the magic sphere, Rule 6 about asking questions with yes or no answers. Rule 8 weighed heavily as he switched his line of vision to contemplate the ball with the 8: *WISELY choose the question you ask the 8 Ball.* He meditated on how to word the query, closed his eyes, prayed, wiggled his fingers at the Magic 8 Ball, took a deep breath, and asked, "What should I do?"

Marry Meg, Bonehead.

* * *

"Way to go, big bro!" Jake slapped Bryce on the back and took the cue stick. "What a run! Maybe you'll have just as good luck with Cornhole or Skee-Ball!"

"Perhaps, li'l bro," Bryce said as Meg approached. "But I am guessing, my fine, young master of ceremonies, that *I'll* soon be *summoned* to have a glass of wine with *my* wife first."

"Whoa, man. Good point. I better find Dawn!"

Meg ambled to the pool table, placed her hand in a corner pocket, withdrew the eight ball, sat it on the baize, and spun it. Without taking her eyes from the twirling black ball, she slowly moved around the table toward Bryce. After she arrived at her destination, she gathered her husband's hands in hers, smiled, and melted him with her eyes and broad smile.

Meg kissed Bryce on the lips and said, "I wish I had the chance to meet Grace, you know? I wish she were here. In our lives with us."

Bryce took Meg in his arms, rested his head against hers, and whispered, "Meg. I don't know how, but she is…Grace is."

Douglas S. Levine applies medical experiences as a physician to his writing. He owns a Magic 8 Ball and swears its use is exclusively recreational. As one who trusts that those who pass on stay with us forever, Doug is grateful "The Gifts of Grace" is part of *Something Extraordinary*.

In Flight

— *Debbie Kaiman Tillinghast*

One day I wrote of clouds and sea as I looked down from above,
I saw a beach with rippled sand, and I held hands with love.
What would I find if I reached that shore?
A whisper of wind or breakers galore, that pounded with a deafening roar?
Lost in drifts of purest white, I wandered on as we flew before the night.
What are the stories of those nearby who journey now with me?
Do they too look out and see the sand, beside a deep blue sea?
Or now transformed to whipped cream mounds atop a fluffy pie,
That make me long to dip a spoon and taste as we wing by?
We glide into a river of gold and I wonder what the next stop holds,
As we leave behind the flaxen light and fly into the sun's good night.
I imagine how it feels to soar through forests glowing bright
Beneath a pillar of soft moonlight, into a sky so real.
I see before me a land aglow with mountain peaks and valleys low,
And I envision a world where I could go to roam through castles made of snow,

Telling my stories of long ago, as day slips into night,

Then I see shapes that have never been, and I let my dreams ascend,

Like the rise of a departing flight.

Debbie Kaiman Tillinghast has been published in *Country* magazine and her poetry has been featured in all ten ARIA anthologies. Debbie, a retired teacher and nutrition educator, now enjoys volunteering as well as writing, gardening, walking and spending time with her children and grandchildren.

The Promise of Gold

— *Peter J. Larrivee*

A late August storm had drenched the sleepy town, and on its heels came a sudden heat wave that covered all of Basherton, Maine in a wet, woolen layer of muggy heat. The best way to cool off was the public pool in the center of town, but that's not where Ethan was heading with Jamie. Instead, the two pedaled their bikes along an old, shady back country road where dust danced in the haze and polluted the blazing sunlight. Jamie had said they were going to the lake, where there would likely be no people to bother them, but Ethan had tried, and failed, to explain that there would also be no girls there as opposed to the public pool, which typically had many.

They were both seventeen, and Ethan had been eager to cool off from the unreasonable heat *and* meet some pretty girls in bathing suits. It seemed Jamie had a different agenda. Not for the first time, Ethan wondered why he even spent time with Jamie. Jamie liked to pull stunts like this, promise one thing, deliver another, and not tell Ethan until the last minute. Ethan thought about bailing on Jamie, but the kid barely had any friends as it was. He was often quiet, told jokes that only seemed funny to him, and in general seemed to stare at people just a little longer than was comfortable. And Jamie had this smug superiority about him, one that was full of confidence and bravado, but at the same time, a kind of pitiable fragility. Jamie was stick-thin, and pale enough that Ethan could understand why he might not want to disrobe in front of other people. In contrast, Ethan was thoroughly suntanned from many hours outside, and had developed some not insignificant muscle, from Boy Scout hikes, from track and field, from swimming. Though in terms of the dynamic between them, somehow Ethan felt lesser than Jamie. It was as if the scrawny boy had some sway over people, himself included.

Very few doors were ever closed to him. That's half the reason Ethan ever went along with him. While not really rich, Jamie's parents spoiled him rotten with material goods that he would lavish on others selectively, for companionship and favors, when he couldn't use his silvered tongue and golden words to convince people to let him into places that were forbidden, or to do things they normally wouldn't. Sometimes he seemed to do it just to prove he could.

Ethan had asked if Jamie wanted to get them passes to the public pool and instead wound up getting talked into an excursion to the lake. Really, it was more of a reservoir, huge, rippling water with gentle, lapping waves that would at least do to cool them off, despite the decided lack of girls.

Their bikes cruised along ruts of dust, hazy in the early afternoon heat, and the sun was unforgiving between the cooling canopy of massive pines, oaks, and maple trees. Ethan was glad for the intermittent shade, but the wind brushing past him was still like a hair dryer, and carried a mass he struggled to push through. He longed for the cool waters that awaited them. He could just imagine leaping off the beach and into the clear gentle water, scaring all the fish away and removing the leaden weight heaped upon him by the weather. The rivulets of sweat running down his body, pooling in unpleasant ways and places, were distracting and seemed to collect the dancing dust to form a thin grime all over his face. He kept slowing down to wipe his face with his shirt. Eventually he outright discarded it, stopping to tie the useless, soaked garment around the handlebars. He stuck his cell phone in with the soiled cotton, to keep it out of the sun and his stream of sweat. Shortly he'd be leaping into cool waters anyway, and didn't want to ruin the phone. He wasn't sure he'd care enough to remember it when they got there, at this rate. He pounded a quick drink from his water bottle before kicking back into the pedals and struggling to catch up to Jamie.

The dirt road turned into a trail, and soon Ethan was bouncing on rough ground, dodging sharp rocks that burst from the worn, dry soil. Ahead of him, Jamie came to a slow stop. Ethan slid up behind him and hopped off the bike.

"Are we close?" Ethan asked, his tone impatient. This was the kind of woods he considered 'tick country,' and it had been a rough summer already, hot and muggy like today, so the crawlies would be out in force. He didn't care to expose himself to more of the little parasites, and it was always on the forefront of his mind from his days at camp.

"Real close," said Jamie with a grin. Ethan knew that grin. He'd seen it before when Jamie suggested going to the lake instead of the pool, or the time Jamie tricked him into stealing by sliding something into his backpack when he wasn't looking. That grin said he was lying about something, and he was internally gloating about having tricked Ethan.

"Jamie, where are we?" Ethan asked, his voice dripping with irritation as he dripped with sweat.

"Don't be a pussy," said Jamie. "We're almost there."

The taunt was enough to get Ethan to steel his resolve and follow after Jamie as he led Ethan out into a small field. They were on foot now, pushing the bikes along as the terrain was a little too rocky to ride on. The grass was tall and overgrown (tick country!), and Jamie was headed for a big pile of rocks in the middle of the field. Ethan could see a part in the tree line on the other side of the field, likely where the lake was, and could almost feel a sense of relief, as if he was mere inches from the abatement of the oppressive humidity. The open air held the muggy haze in stark contrast to the promised relief below.

Jamie stopped at the pile of rocks and climbed up onto the top of the biggest boulder. He gestured down at the pile beneath him, his arms splayed dramatically, as if he'd just conquered the new world.

"Behold!" he said, dramatically.

Ethan just stared at him. "What? The rocks?"

"Not just rocks," said Jamie with his smirk returning. "We're on the site of the Harrison Gold Mine!"

Again, all Ethan could do was stare. He made a 'go on' gesture with his hand, eager to get to the point, or more importantly, the lake.

"Harrison Gold Mine," said Jamie. "Back in 1870, Arnold Harrison found a rich gold vein in some quartz on this very spot. He dug a mine about a hundred feet deep and mined it all out. But when he tried to dig for more veins, he came up empty and gave up. So, he put some of the rocks back on top of the shaft and got old, and died."

"Jamie, I could be surrounded by girls in bikinis right now," said Ethan, angrily.

"Oh, you'll have plenty of those once we find the gold."

"You said they mined out all the gold," Ethan snapped.

"In 1870! Think about it, what did they have back then? Pickaxes and shovels. They used really crude methods to dig it out. Chances are, they missed a lot of it. And maybe it wasn't worth *their* time to go looking for more, but we have nothing to lose. Anything we find is pure profit. All we have to do is look for some granite and quartz, and we'll find some gold. Real gold! Even a little bit of gold is worth a lot of money right now. And even if we don't find much, we'll be famous just for finding any."

"Where do you get this stuff?"

"The internet."

"Oh, then it must be true."

"There're all kinds of unrecorded history around here. Just think of what we could find if we tried. Gold, or like, old artifacts or something. Indian totems?"

Ethan stepped up onto the rock pile, more to be out of the tall grass than anything else. One of the stones seemed to sink a bit as he stepped on it, and the ground beneath felt soft, possibly from the previous night's torrential storm, but he made it to a stable section and looked back to Jamie. He considered Jamie's idea, which sounded to him like picking through rocks on a hot day, instead of cooling off at the lake. The idea had zero appeal, especially since Jamie's smug grin of satisfaction probably had less to do with the prospect of finding gold, and more to do with the amusement of getting under Ethan's skin.

"If we pick up some rocks, can we take them to the water to examine them? I'm sweating buckets here."

Jamie grinned, nodding his head. "Of course. Anything you want," he lied.

What, or rather who, Ethan wanted was probably sunning her lithe body at the public pool before another dip, but he was already here, and the lake was right there. It seemed easier to just pick up some rocks and head towards the lake. He could leave Jamie to play geologist while he cooled off. On the way back, he considered ditching Jamie and swinging by Freezee's ice cream to see if he could run into anyone there.

"Okay," said Ethan, who bent down to grab a rock that looked nicely portable.

"No no," said Jamie. "What you want is granite, like…like this." He picked up a rock, a heavy one judging from the way his arms strained, so heavy he fumbled it and it fell onto the pile again, making a cracking sound as it collided with another stone, and landed with a deep thud at the base of the pile. The whole pile shifted under their feet, and Ethan had just enough time to notice the sudden change in the air, and the vanishing light before tumbling into the cold dark.

***

Ethan bounced off dirt and rock until he rolled to a stop in near total darkness. He couldn't tell which way was up, but the faint shadows he could see gave him the impression that he was in some kind of cave. He wheezed for a moment, struggling for air, like his chest couldn't get enough breath in it. He felt wetness on his elbows and head, turning grimy with the dirt that now coated him. Still dizzy from the fall, it took him a moment to realize where they'd landed.

He didn't understand how, and he didn't want to believe it had even happened, but here he was, deep underground. The air was cool and dry, enough to even make him shiver. He stood up, and felt pain in his knee, and his arm felt scraped and banged up. The pain was raw, reminding him of when he'd torn a muscle in Little League, or when he sprained his ankle on a hike at summer camp. Only it hit him from several places at once, and he couldn't help letting out a groan.

"Ethan?" came Jamie's voice. It sounded far away and strained, like he was similarly hurt. Jamie reacted to pain like a vampire to garlic. Ethan always felt sorry for him when he heard that childlike pleading in his voice, which may have been the only thing that kept him from punching the kid in situations like this.

"Yeah?" said Ethan, forcing his voice though limited breath. "Jamie?" He coughed on the dust that flooded in as he struggled to pull in breath.

"Ethan, help! I think I broke my leg!"

Ethan reached out and steadied himself on a rocky wall. If Jamie's leg was broken, there was no way Ethan could lift him out, even if he could climb up the shaft. He wasn't a lifter, like some of the gym rats that lingered in the weight room after class. Ethan looked up. The shaft seemed to go on for miles, the daylight at the top nothing but a jagged hole, white against the gloom.

"Where are you?" Ethan asked.

"Right here!" Jamie cried.

Ethan turned in the direction, but his hands met hard, warm stone, like stone that had been in the sun all day. Ethan slowly put it together. This was the boulder Jamie had been standing on. It was a miracle it hadn't crushed either of them, or worse. Jamie had to be on the other side of it; the mass of the rocks kept them on their respective sides. Ethan tried to climb over it, but it had no hand holds, and even when he got near the top, his head banged against a low ceiling. He fell back to the cold earth.

"You idiot," Ethan hissed, partly to himself.

If Ethan wanted to get out, he'd need to find another way. Even if he could have squeezed through the opening, he'd never get back up the shaft.

"Jamie, is there another way out of here?"

"What?" Jamie asked.

"Another way out? A shaft that doesn't go straight up, maybe?"

Jamie whimpered, "I…I don't know." He was blubbering now, like a small hurt child instead of the cocky, arrogant teen he was. His breath came in ragged sobs. Ethan actually felt bad for him, again. Hurt, nearly alone, in the dark. But Jamie had spent a lot of time calling Ethan a pussy and forcing him to prove himself; now he sat in the dirt crying. A certain irritation built, but he pushed it aside. There wasn't much else he could do. He could berate Jamie for being so stupidly impulsive, for dragging him away from his own comfort zone to go chasing gold, but ultimately it would leave them both still trapped, underground. Even still, Ethan wanted to get beyond the boulder and give that broken leg a kick, just to drive the point home. What if they couldn't get out? Nobody knew where they were. If there was no way out, then what?

"Okay, well," said Ethan, "I can't get to you over this boulder. I need to find a way out and go get help."

"Where's your phone?!" Jamie cried.

"With my bike! Where's yours?!" Ethan snapped, losing his forced composure. "I was planning to go jump in a lake!"

Jamie whimpered some more, letting out deep sobs. Ethan's guilt rose up to counter his anger. Jamie might have gotten him into something stupid, but he was still hurt, and still pathetic underneath all his facade. Jamie's phone was probably broken, but Ethan didn't push.

"Okay, okay, I'm sorry," Ethan said. "Look, just…just keep it together. Let me see what I can find. I'm gonna go this way and try to find a way out."

*

Ethan groped along rough stone away from the shaft. The small amount of light diminished fast, leaving him unsure if the vague shapes in front of him were his hands, or his imagination. He walked with his arms outstretched, his feet not straying too far from the ground, and he moved slowly so he didn't trip on anything, or worse yet, find the edge of another shaft or crevasse and go tumbling down again.

He kept checking the proximity of the wall, too, groping in utter silence and darkness. He couldn't help being angry at Jamie as the reality of the situation fell upon him. Once again, he found himself in trouble because of one of Jamie's idiot ideas. "Gold," Ethan grumbled under his breath. Even if there was any gold to be found, he didn't expect they would find it, and Jamie was either too dumb to know that, or too greedy to care. Maybe it wasn't even about that. Maybe the kid just got off on convincing Ethan to do something he didn't want to do.

Ethan felt his foot sink a little deeper into the dirt, and a wet sensation pooled around him. It was some kind of mud or muck. He grimaced and pulled his foot from the mess. He gently prodded the ground with his foot and found it was turning into a muddy mess ahead of him. He badly wished he had some kind of light to be able to see what was ahead. He hoped it didn't get very muddy. While the cold sludge provided some relief to his aches, it was not a pleasant thought to sink into something he couldn't climb out of. He put his foot forward again and gradually put more weight on it until it seemed to sink to a fixed point. It only went in an inch or so as far as he could tell. He braved another step.

More muck. Another step, carefully, holding on to the wall. It seemed like the stone was sweating; a sheen of moisture coated the rock now. Step, step, the muck began to get deeper, and suddenly, Ethan was splashing into water. It was some kind of underground pool. The water was cold, refreshing, but probably murky and stagnant. He took careful steps. He didn't want to get any in his mouth. The water rose higher, soon at his waist. He was grateful he'd worn the swim trunks, but his sandals were now lost in the mud, and he took barefoot steps, blind in the wet earth.

His next step felt purchase, but only for a moment, and mid-step the mud gave way, sinking beneath him. Ethan fell into the wet water, thrashing his arms to catch himself. His arm slid off the wet stone wall, and he submerged.

He couldn't tell if his eyes were open or closed, but he could swear there was something within his vision in that murk. He surfaced for a breath, treading water as the muddy floor beneath him seemed to give away entirely. He took several breaths, throwing back his wet hair, before sucking in a deep breath and sliding into the dark.

***

He was more sure of it now, some vague light, like sunlight breaking through clouds. It wasn't very far; he should be able to reach it if he swam full out.

He pushed himself forward, and soon the faint brown light that broke the pitch told of a surface to the water. He could not have gone far; his breath was still held with no problem.

Breaking the surface, the world turned bitterly cold.

He struggled up slimy stone to get purchase in a dim, earthen hollow. Roots dangled from above, and massive stone slabs made an uneven floor. The light seemed to be coming from a break in the hollow at the water level, where the blistering summer sun made a tiny invasion. It wasn't big enough for him to get through, but maybe it could be. It looked to be mostly dirt; maybe he could dig through it with his hands. Once out on the lake, he could go back and get help for Jamie.

Suddenly the sun he'd been so desperate to escape was a beacon, its warmth and light calling to him, promising safety and hope.

Ethan slid back into the water and towards the hole. He poked at the dirt, found it was very hard-packed, but the water made it a little easier to scrape away. He started to work on the hole and managed to clear a large chunk of sludge. Light poured in now, and Ethan had to turn away to shield his eyes. They'd become so used to the dark, he felt physical pain beholding simple daylight.

He waited for his sun-blighted vision to clear, turning away back towards the hollow. From that angle, and with the increased light, some of the thick dangling roots looked different. He could almost see them as dangling fingers. He rubbed his eyes and tried to get them to stop hurting. He wiped water and muck from them and focused on what he was seeing.

He looked back to find what he had taken for a straight root was a skeletal arm, coated in thin black mud, several fingers missing, and held in some kind of shape by tattered fabric. He jumped back, looking at the dangling roots around him. It wasn't a singular arm. Here and there, in some cases intertwined with roots, many arms, legs, even skulls dangled and stared at him with sockets full of black earth. Finger bones dripped from the sudden motion, landing in the waters that Ethan had thrashed in. One of the disjointed bodies had a thick worm crawling through exposed ribs. The labyrinthine network of roots had grown around, into the bones over decades, and woven them into the earth and the surrounding stone. A hanging jawbone from a small skull twisted idly, a toddler's skull, with exposed adult teeth beneath the baby teeth, lying in wait to grow and burrow up into the gums that had long ago rotted away. Half-dangling bodies of incomplete skeletons hung above him, suspended only by roots and rocks, the ancient bones lurking above, the empty skulls watched him as he flailed back from the gaze of the uncountable dead. Large hands held things that looked like rusted knives, or old rotted leather bags. The graveyard above him almost seemed to be reaching down for him in that tiny dark hollow, threatening to descend upon him as gravity dictated they should. He screamed and slid beneath the black water, only to feel sharp pokes of sticks or roots, bones, rocks, he couldn't be sure. But it felt as if the scattered dead were reaching for him.

He surfaced and choked out the necrotic water around him. Ethan desperately clawed at the ground around that singular point of light, clawing with his hands and screaming, choking, gasping for air while he pulled handfuls of mud away, pushing forward and clawing like an animal. He barely noticed his fingers were cut, bruised, banged up on rocks and roots during his feral terror. His arms reached forward in a desperate scramble, as if to grab fistfuls of salvation.

Finally, he pushed himself through the gap, and with some pan-icked twisting, he fell forward into the cool waters of the lake, barely remembering to suck in a lungful of air before crashing into the open waters.

***

Ethan remained under for a moment, until he was sure he was out of the hollow, until he was positive the sun was above him, push-ing through murky cold.

He broke the surface, the air almost thick enough to choke on, and in his desperation, he sucked in a few droplets that landed in his throat, causing him to cough and sputter while his manic thrashing threw curtains of water all around him. His feet reached bottom at some point, and the secure footing helped him catch his breath.

He wiped the hair and water out of his eyes, turning back to look at the hole he'd escaped from. It was one small rise in a whole area of untouched lakefront. A few trees struggled to grow up from it, their roots tangled into the mass, keeping its shape intact, but the trunks bent at odd angles, jutting outward, reaching for the light above and growing in wild curves like the hillside was a massive bubble that took centuries to form. Nobody would think there were bodies buried there, nobody would even think there was an old hidden graveyard. Or worse, was this some kind of mass grave? Ethan had swum in the lake since he was five. People had come to the lake since people existed, before the public pool opened. It had shoreline enough for everyone to share, and no one was the wiser that they swam with the dead.

Ethan pushed himself towards a different shore, something more stable, easier to climb, and far away from the dangling bones.

He trudged through the woods until he found the clearing again. There were the bikes they'd left in the tall grass, and there was the hole opened up by soft mud and time. He stepped as close to the hole as he dared.

"Jamie!" he shouted down.

"Ethan?! Where are you?!"

"Out," he said. "I'm going to get help."

"Don't leave me again!" cried the pathetic wail.

"What am I supposed to do? Fly down there?!"

"Ethan, I'm…I'm scared!"

He wanted to scream at Jamie, even with the desperation in his cry. He wanted to just walk away and leave him in that hole. Jamie had brought him there, promised him gold, and all he found were the bones of the dead.

He wanted to be cruel. He felt he was more than right to be cruel in that moment.

"Help is coming," Ethan shouted down the hole. "Just stay there, and don't move."

He started walking. Part of him wanted to throw more rocks down there. That wasn't who he was, though. That was more like what Jamie would do. Jamie would laugh. Jamie would throw rocks down and tease him for being scared.

But Ethan picked up his bike, and pushed himself back through the woods, and followed the power lines to the nearest house.

***

It took all day for rescuers to pull Jamie out of the hole. The local news had a quick blurb about it. Ethan told the police about the hollow with the buried bodies. They searched the area around the lake but couldn't find anything that matched his description. Nobody was willing to venture into the old shaft itself, and it was quietly filled in with soil so there couldn't be any more accidents.

Ethan didn't see Jamie for over a month, and he was glad. But when he did see that pale, scrawny, little shit with the lying grin, he turned right around and walked the other way. No golden promises would be enough to sway him now.

Peter J. Larrivee is a horror/fantasy author who hails from the Land of Lovecraft. Look for his other books online or at select shops and bookstores around Rhode Island.

www.ingramcontent.com/pod-product-compliance
Lightning Source LLC
Chambersburg PA
CBHW060624260626
47161CB00008B/2792